Are You Or

A Video Arts Gui

Video Arts is the world's leading producer and distributor of training videos. There are now over 150 Video Arts titles in daily use by some 100,000 organisations worldwide, spread throughout 60 countries. Between them they have won over 200 awards in major international festivals.

Video Arts programmes combine the highest standards of production excellence with the maximum training impact. The quality of research, writing, activity and production is exceptional, and the 'So You Think You Can Manage' series is designed to make available this expertise, entertainment and long-established success in handy book form.

Are You Organised?

Video Arts

*Cartoons by Shaun Williams,
and Carlo Roberto*

Mandarin

This book is based on the following Video Arts training videos:

The Unorganised Manager I–IV
   The Unorganised Manager – Damnation
   The Unorganised Manager – Salvation
   The Unorganised Manager – Lamentations
   The Unorganised Manager – Revelations
When Can You Start?
The Paper Chase
The Business Letter Business

A Mandarin Paperback
ARE YOU ORGANISED?

First published in Great Britain 1994
by Mandarin Paperbacks
an imprint of Reed Consumer Books Ltd
Michelin House, 81 Fulham Road, London SW3 6RB
and Auckland, Melbourne, Singapore and Toronto

Copyright © Video Arts Ltd 1994
Illustrations © Video Arts Ltd

A CIP catalogue record for this title
is available from the British Library
ISBN 0 7493 1832 5

Printed and bound in Great Britain
by Cox & Wyman Ltd, Reading, Berkshire

Contents

1 The unorganised manager – Damnation

The first principle of management is this:

If you cannot manage yourself you cannot manage anyone.

We are all familiar with the picture of the harassed, overworked executive: there is a mountainous in-tray; his or her appointments are double-booked; there is a bulging briefcase to take home after hours – in every way a suitable case for a coronary.

Yet such a person will have at least one comfort – they know they are doing a Good Job. The company depends on them; they are loved and needed by their colleagues . . . But is this true? Let us start by looking at how one manager – we will call him Richard – performs.

Richard Lewis is in Food. He is an Area Manager in charge of half a dozen District Managers; but despite his responsibilities he never lets them get in the way of his goodwill, his ever-open door, his good intentions, his willingness to take on all problems, big and small. His behaviour is repeated countless times at all levels of all companies and organisations. Here he is at work with his long-suffering secretary Ginnie, and taking a telephone call from Bernard, one of his District Managers:

> **Richard:** Yes, Bernard, of course I understand, yes I realise that, you're the Catering Manager . . . well, why not mushroom soup *today* and tomato soup *tomorrow*? . . . Good . . . Fine, 'bye.
> **Ginnie:** What's wrong?
> **Richard:** I don't know, he always seems to need me

to sort things out. Still, that's what I'm here for.
Now, where were we?
Ginnie: We were doing this letter.
Richard: Ah yes, how far had we got?
Ginnie: 'Dear Mr Johnson . . .'
Richard: . . . Was that it? Right! 'Dear Mr
Johnson . . .'

But Keith, a colleague, rushes in. Richard *always* keeps
an open door.

Keith: Oh Richard – got a minute?
Richard: Ah, Keith. Yes, come on in.
Keith: You haven't got a cup of coffee handy, have
you?
Richard: Yes, sure. Ginnie, get Keith a cup of
coffee. Me too, while you're at it.
Ginnie: Milk and sugar?
Keith: Oh, no sugar for me, thank you. Calories.
Lovely girl. Very tasty.
Richard: Er . . . was there something in particular
you wanted, Keith?
Keith: What? Oh yes, yes there was actually. It's
about my daughter's twenty-first birthday party. I'm
getting a bit worried. We arranged that I'd organise
the marquee and the suppliers say they can't do
anything for the weekend.
Richard: Oh well, I'll see what I can do.

Richard, always willing, dials immediately.

Richard: Hello. Is that Under-Canvas? Yes, it's
Richard Lewis here . . . yes, that's right, I'm the
Area Manager of Parker and Gibbs Catering. I
understand there's a problem about a marquee for us
on Saturday week . . .

One of Richard's phones starts to ring.

Richard: Oh look – can you hang on a minute, my other phone's going? Hullo, oh Bernard, can you hang on a minute? I've got Keith, the Vending Manager with me, I'm at a meeting and I'm on the other line – look Bernard, I can't talk now. I'll hand you over to Ginnie, all right? Look, Ginnie, can you take this? He says it's urgent.

So Richard has sorted out the soup crisis, is busy attending to Keith's daughter's marquee, has left Ginnie to deal with Bernard's urgent phone call and, if he has time for thought, will be silently repeating 'that's what I'm here for'. Let's see what happens as Richard gets on with his job.

Richard: Hello, hello, you will do your very best for us, won't you? It's for Keith's daughter, you see. It's her twenty-first.

Ginnie: *Can't* you possibly talk to Bernard, he says . . .

Richard: I'll phone him back later, I told you.

Ginnie: Bernard, he says he'll phone you back. I'm sorry. 'Bye.

Richard: She's called Karen, yes, she's a sweet kid . . . Yes, so I'll be hearing from you then? Oh, they've hung up! Well, I think it'll be all right, Keith.

Keith: Oh great. Thanks, Richard.

Ginnie: Bernard's got a crisis down at Bexley.

Richard: What sort of crisis?

Ginnie: Meat deliveries haven't arrived, staff haven't turned up and he's discovered some pilfering.

Richard: Oh Lord! Well, what did you say?

Ginnie: I said I'd tell you.

Richard: . . . Well, is that all?

Ginnie: What else? I tried . . .

Richard: What else? Ginnie, have I got to do *everything*? Sorry, I didn't mean to snap. Get him on the phone, will you?

Keith: Well, I think I'd better leave you to it then. Thanks for the coffee.

Chaos is contagious

Keith leaves the scene of confusion, oblivious to the fact that his request has helped to create it. After all, it's always like that in Richard's office. Of course several vital things have been accomplished that afternoon: the colour of tomorrow's soup has been agreed; some progress on the marquee is in train; a nice cup of coffee has been drunk. Naturally one or two matters have unavoidably been left in the air . . .

Richard: What's happening?

Ginnie: No reply.

Richard: Why doesn't he reply? Bernard can't blow his nose without consulting me.

Ginnie: He said he *had* to talk to you because he can't sack one of the kitchen porters for pilfering without your OK.

Richard: Oh. I see. Still no reply? Well, look, you'd better trot off now. But try and get this call through to Bernard.

Ginnie: But what about your letter?

Richard: What letter?

Ginnie: To Mr Johnson. You said it was vital.

Richard: It *is* vital, it's about the new contract at the Royal Victoria Hall. We're opening up there on site in seven weeks . . . send it off right away.

Ginnie: Well, you haven't finished it.

Richard: How far have we got?

Ginnie: 'Dear Mr Johnson . . .'

Richard is not destined to get far, for at that moment Eric, a newly appointed District Manager, comes in to see his boss. Richard is nonplussed, but welcoming as ever.

Richard: Ah, Eric, Eric, come in, come in. Sit down. Now, what can I do for you?

Eric: Well . . . you asked me to pop in and see you.

Richard: Did we have an appointment? Sorry . . . Why isn't it in the diary, Ginnie? Ah, here it is. Oh yes, Monday's the day you start as District Manager, isn't it?

Eric: Yes, you said you'd brief me this afternoon.

Richard: Yes, of course. *Get* that flaming phone, would you, Ginnie? I'm at a meeting.

Ginnie: It's the Managing Director's secretary. He's leaving his office and you said you had to talk to him this afternoon.

Richard: It can wait till tomorrow.

Ginnie: He's going abroad tomorrow for the week.

Richard: Tell him I'll catch him on the way down.

Ginnie: Hello – it's all right, he'll catch him on the way down – yes, like he usually does!

Richard: Ah well, Eric, there's nothing else I need tell you really. You're a good chap. You can handle it. Here are your car keys. Off you go!

Eric: But . . . Mr Lewis.

Richard: Twelve contracts in your care. It's a big challenge. Good luck. Anything else you need to know, just ask Ginnie.

Ginnie: What about your call to Bernard?

Richard: Tell him I'll be down tomorrow.

Ginnie: And your letter to Mr Johnson?

Richard: Tomorrow!

Ginnie: But . . .

Richard: Ginnie, I can't do *everything*!

Yes, a thoroughly conscientious character. And a dangerous one. Richard hasn't grasped *that it is easier to be busy than to get things done*. The result, of course, is that nobody surrounding him can get anything done either. His colleagues suffer, and so will his family. He'll never have enough time for them either, with the innumerable reports and memoranda he hasn't dealt with at the office transported nightly to his home. Those who have time for everybody end up with time for nobody. Of all this he is quite oblivious. In his own estimation he will, when he dies (prematurely, of course) be bound straight for the Celestial Executive Suite in the Sky where all Good

Managers repose for eternity. Why not? He has tried his hardest. He deserves the best in after-life. But he will be in for a rude shock, and his reception will be exactly the opposite of what he expects.

Picture what happens. The inevitable coronary has occurred and he finds himself at the Gates of Heaven, confronted by St Peter . . .

> **St Peter:** Hello. Can I help you?
>
> **Richard:** Oh, pleased to meet you. What happens now?
>
> **St Peter:** What did you have in mind?
>
> **Richard:** Well . . . can I come in?
>
> **St Peter:** Come *in*? I'll just check. Oh, sorry . . . I'm afraid you must be due at the other place.
>
> **Richard:** But that's not possible. There must be a mistake. I've lived a good life . . . I've always made time for other people. I've always had an open door, I'm kind and patient, I've tried so hard to do things right, are you sure . . . ?
>
> **St Peter:** You're on record as a classic sinner, I'm sorry to say. A man who does evil while he thinks he's doing good.
>
> **Richard:** Me? But I've always helped everyone. They all like me and appreciate what I've tried to do.
>
> **St Peter:** You really think so? Would you like to see what one or two of them said about you only today?

So St Peter shows him a glimpse of life back on Earth. They listen to Ginnie . . .

> **Ginnie:** He's ghastly to work for. When he's in the office, I'm on edge all day. I never know what's happening or what to do and he'll never let me get on with my work. And when he's not messing me about I can never find him. He's always under pressure and

snapping at me . . .

And Eric . . .

> **Eric:** You just don't know where you are. When I really need his help, he never has time to talk about anything properly. I'm so confused about the job, and I've just got no confidence left . . .

And Bernard . . .

> **Bernard:** And when you *do* get hold of him, he starts doing your job for you, checking everything and changing half of it just for the sake of it. He's absolutely hopeless.

And his wife Cathy:

> **Cathy:** I just hope he's not as appalling to work for as he is to live with – he forgets everything, even birthdays. Says he'll do things and cancels at the last minute because he's never got time. You can never rely on him . . .
> **St Peter:** See?
> **Richard:** I don't believe it . . . where did I go wrong?

St Peter, of course, is right: as an ex-Pope he is infallible. Richard is guilty of self-delusion and doesn't realise that the characteristics he most admires about himself are bad for business, bad for his family, bad for his colleagues, bad for his company and bad for himself. It isn't everybody who gets a second chance, but St Peter is a kindly soul, if that's the right word . . .

> **Richard:** Please – please give me one more chance, *please*.
> **St Peter:** Oh dear, I always dread this bit. All right,

14

but only if you promise to put right all those things which you have done wrong.

Richard: Fine. Er, what exactly?

St Peter: Well, where does one begin? Allowing everyone else to interrupt you. Doing jobs you don't need to do. Not establishing your priorities . . .

Richard: *Priorities?*

St Peter: Priorities. Misusing your secretary, trying to do other people's jobs for them. In other words, wasting your own time and wasting everyone else's.

Richard: I never.

St Peter: Yes you *did*! And you never have enough time for your staff.

Richard: That's not true.

St Peter: Yes it is.

Richard: Well, I'm truly very sorry. But I meant well. And I'll be a different person if I can just have another chance.

St Peter: You mustn't be a different person. You must be the *same* person *organised*.

Richard: I'll try. Thank you. You're an angel.

St Peter: No, just a saint.

Richard has been told a number of office truths – all of them new to him. He has been told to **establish priorities**, that he is supposed to be doing his own job and not other people's. That means, of course, that he has been introduced to the subtle concept of **delegating**, because if he isn't doing other people's jobs, then they have to do them. He has certainly grasped that he has to become more organised. Let us see how he handles his second chance . . .

> **Richard:** 'Morning, Ginnie. Now let's make a really organised start today.

Ginnie: Mr Lewis, are you feeling all right? I heard you were taken ill last night.

Richard: Oh yes, it was nothing, just a heart attack.

Ginnie: Should you be here?

Richard: Yes, I'll be all right. Now, we've got all sorts of things to do today. We must make sure that we've got that marquee for Keith and I must write that letter to Mr Johnson and I want you to ring up Eric and see how he's getting on as District Manager – where's the post, by the way?

Ginnie: Here.

Richard: Anything interesting?

Ginnie: I don't know, we haven't dealt with yesterday's yet.

Richard: Right, well let's do that now as well. Here's yesterday's – in fact, here's the whole pending tray. There's *weeks* of stuff here. Now I want you to take it all, go through it and chuck out anything we've missed the deadline for. Then summarise everything that's there, underlining anything that's vital. And *today's* post. And get Bernard on the phone for me right away . . . what's the matter?

Ginnie: When do you want it done by? In what order?

Richard: I want it all done now. Oh dear, don't be such a ninny, Ginnie. What's wrong now? *Stop crying*!

Not an outstanding success. To make progress, Richard will have to go right back to basics. He has to learn to plan, but also that *you can't learn how to plan if you don't know what to plan. He has to learn that doing your tasks is not the same thing as doing your job.* Above all, he has to know what his own job is. Could you describe yours accurately and succinctly? It is the key to planning. Back in heaven, St Peter realises he has a big job on hand. Nothing less than a complete conversion will do. Richard is summoned back for Instrtuction which alone can lead to Salvation.

Golden rules

1 A door that's always open invites anarchy to walk in.
2 Trying to do everything means nothing is done properly.
3 It's easier to be busy than to get things done.
4 Let others get on with their own jobs.
5 Establishing priorities is a priority.
6 In order to plan you have to know what to plan.
7 Doing your tasks is not the same thing as doing your job.
8 Learn what your job really is.

2 The unorganised manager – Salvation

We've looked at Richard's problems, and they are very considerable. He is busy but not productive, the job he does bear no relation to his real role in the company, his delegation reflects his own lack of organisation. In short, he can't cope because he has never thought to ask himself **what his actual job should be**. He is fortunate that St Peter has his case in hand. A less patient saint would, possibly, consider a second martyrdom preferable.

St Peter: You are the most unorganised person I know. Why don't you ever plan anything?
Richard: I do . . . Well, I haven't got time for planning.
St Peter: Without planning, you'll never have time for anything.
Richard: Look, I can't sit around planning what to do. I have to get on and *do* it. I'm harassed, overworked and I haven't got the time – why do you think I had that coronary?
St Peter: As a matter of fact, we arranged that, to give your colleagues a bit of a break. Now stop panicking, sit down and listen. You must take control of your time and decide what you're going to spend it on. You must spend your time as carefully as you spend your money. It's a budget item. And an expensive one. Remember, you only have a finite amount of time – down there, anyway.
Richard: I see.

St Peter: Now. What are you down there for? What are you employed for?

Richard: Well, to check on my District Managers, do appraisals of subordinates and liaise with Finance.

St Peter: No, that's what you *do*. What is your purpose? Your purpose, you toy executive, is to provide quality food at prices your clients can afford while maximising your profit margin. Am I correct?

Richard: Well, if you put it like that, yes. That is the company's purpose.

St Peter: Therefore it's yours. And to do it you need to **control your time** properly. Start by making a list of all the jobs you've got to get done.

Richard: What should be first?

St Peter: Write down everything, in any order. We'll sort them out later.

Richard: Right . . . well, let's see, there's Keith's marquee, my letter to Mr Johnson, the clients' trading accounts, organise the agricultural show, look at the new XG vending machine, renegotiate next year's contract with Bradley's, get tickets for the Health, Safety and Hygiene Conference, sort out Bernard's problem . . . My God, there's a hell of a lot to do. I'd better get on with it.

St Peter: *Not yet*! . . . Now sort those tasks into two categories. The active positive tasks and the reactive tasks. It's all right, I'll explain. Always remember that the **active positive tasks** are the ones that help you to achieve the objectives of your job. The **reactive tasks** are all the junk that lands on your desk every day that you have to deal with to keep things running.

Richard: I see. Well – active positive tasks: organise the agricultural show, renegotiate next year's contract

The reactive tasks are all the junk that lands on your desk

with Bradley's . . .
St Peter: That's it. The active positive tasks are the ones that help you to build the business – to get more contracts and to make more profit on the ones you've already got. The reactive tasks, those are the everyday running problems. So sort the tasks into those two categories. Now, to plan your time properly, you must **schedule each task** properly.
Richard: *Schedule?*

St Peter: Yes, and before you schedule a task, you need to know two things about it. One, how long you want to spend on it, which is determined by how **important** it is. Two, how soon you need to get it done by, which is determined by how **urgent** it is. Importance and urgency are not the same thing. An urgent task is *not* necessarily important. It may be urgent but trivial – in which case do it straight away, but spend only a very few minutes on it, thereby leaving yourself lots of time for the important tasks. Positive active tasks are nearly always important. Reactive tasks are very often not important. So, judge the importance of each task by reference to that. *Then*, quite separately, deal with the matter of its urgency.

Richard: Suppose it's urgent and important?

St Peter: Then you deal with it straight away, and you give it a lot of time. It's not difficult! So when you sit down to schedule your time . . .

Richard: In my appointments diary?

St Peter: In your appointments diary . . . block in big spaces of time for the important tasks – probably active positive ones – while leaving enough space for all the reactive ones that are going to land on your desk every day, a lot of which will be urgent but trivial. Goodbye.

Richard: . . . I'm not quite sure I've got it.

St Peter: All right, Ginnie will show you.

Richard: Ginnie!

St Peter: I shall personally inspire her. I haven't the time to train earthlings, I've got eternity to manage.

*Ask yourself which is the more important, Mr Sidgewick –
closing the Saudi deal, or designing a stretch cover
for your sellotape dispenser . . .*

Establish your priorities

Priorities, scheduling his time, distinguishing between
the urgent and important, discovering that tasks can be
active and reactive, learning that his job is what his
company is about, not necessarily what he is actually
doing, making plans to ensure that things get done in
the right order . . . poor Richard! However, St Peter
keeps his promise and so a divinely inspired Ginnie gets
to work:

Richard: Any ideas, Ginnie?
Ginnie: Well, so we can leave lots of time for
important tasks, why don't we deal with reactive ones
like normal people . . . no offence . . . first they open
the letters, in the *morning*.
Richard: Do they?

Ginnie: Then they dictate replies immediately, or decide what action to take and actually take it, if you follow my meaning . . . And they allow space for that in the appointments diary every morning.

Richard: Every morning? How long?

Ginnie: Half an hour?

Richard: That's a good idea. Half an hour every morning to react to the post. And then there's Eric. I must go out and see that he's doing all right, he's only just started as District Manager. So that takes care of this morning. Then I could pop back and see Bernard and drop in on a couple of sites – oh and fix that light switch . . .

Ginnie: Why not spend the whole day with Eric?

Richard: A whole day?

Ginnie: Yes, it's important, isn't it?

Richard: But what about my other managers?

Ginnie: Give them each a whole day.

Richard: *Each* a whole day? But that's practically the whole week gone!

Ginnie: No. What about one next week and one the week after?

Richard: Next week. Yes. There's a week next week, isn't there? That's true. That's an active task. I can schedule that in ahead of time. And I could leave some time free every day in case they wanted to talk to me in the meantime.

Ginnie: Great!

Richard: Oh that's fine, fine. OK, is that the diary done?

Ginnie: Well, didn't you want to see the Managing Director in his office?

Richard: Oh yes, you'd better fix up an appointment later.

Ginnie: Better do it now.

But it can't be done now. Again Keith, always sure of that welcome, bursts in.

Keith: Richard, got a minute?
Richard: Ah, Keith, yes, come in, come in, sit down.
Keith: Thanks. Gosh, what a terrible journey into work, traffic all the way, a great big articulated lorry had jackknifed and caused a two-mile jam. There was . . .

Then Richard hears a Voice . . .

St Peter: Is this important? Essential for your work?

And responds sharply:

Richard: Keith, do you really mean a minute?
Keith: Eh?
Richard: I have got a *minute*, but if you want longer we'll have to do it later.
Keith: Oh well, no, not really, I just wanted to know about my marquee.
Richard: I'm chasing that up this morning. Anything else? No? Good. That's fine, lovely. Well, look, it's been very nice to see you.
Keith: Have I . . . upset you in some way, old chap?
Richard: No.
Ginnie: Wednesday afternoon?
Richard: Ah yes, I'm keeping Wednesday afternoons free, you know, in case things crop up. You could drop in then.
Keith: Oh, great. Fine. See you then.

Exit Keith.

Richard: Well done, Ginnie.

Ginnie: Shall I put your available time in the appointments diary then, and notify everyone?
Richard: Notify them?
Ginnie: Tell them that's when you're available to see them – so they realise when you're *not*.
Richard: Realise when I'm not available? Oh happiness! Oh, Ginnie, you're a tower of strength. Now then, let me see, just a minute, there's nothing down there for Thursday. *It's completely wasted.*
Ginnie: That's your time for long-term discussions, to improve next year's profits.
Richard: What discussions?
Ginnie: Where we're going, future plans. And I've allowed fifteen minutes at the end of each day to co-ordinate the diaries and make out tomorrow's list. And I've got bring-forward files, a wall chart and a year planner.
Richard: What for?
Ginnie: Long-term scheduling. For your regular meetings. So you don't have to remember anything, and you can see things at a glance.

It's that Voice again.

St Peter: So what do you do after you've made your list and established your priorities?
Richard: I schedule my time in my appointments diary.
St Peter: And how do you divide it up?
Richard: I schedule the positive active tasks – the things I'm here for – leaving time for the reactive tasks – the problems that crop up from day to day.
St Peter: *Now* you have organised yourself! Hallelujah!

Ginnie has opened a new world for Richard – a world of properly kept diaries, 'to do' lists, bring-forward files and visual planners. Let's look at these in more detail.

The diary should not be a repository of 'reactive' appointments and dates. Constructively used, it should be a tool for the future in which time for planning, time for your own availability for others – and of course non-availability – the scheduling of important tasks which need time to be set aside for them, regular meetings with colleagues which could well go by default through simply not ensuring that they happen, etc. etc., are enshrined.

A 'to do' list isn't a mere jumble of immediate problems. It should be a guide in itself to those tasks which are active and reactive, important and trivial, urgent and not urgent. Some of the most important tasks – the active ones concerned with your real job – will sit on that list for weeks, provided that the requisite time is laid aside for actually accomplishing them in an effective manner.

Bring-forward files can be like a second memory – almost certainly better than your first! A regular reminder of tasks which are 'pending' (probably they will be pending because they require something else to happen before you can deal with them) can be an essential piece of office equipment.

Visual planners accurately and regularly updated can save hours of leafing through ill-assorted figures and reports. Whether they are used for production schedules, staff holidays or whatever, once they are at work they will be working for you.

Finally Ginnie has introduced Richard to a proper use of his secretary. She knows her job and wants to be left to get on with it; she also wants to help him do his, but has had to wait until he knows what his job is before she can be properly confident in her own. Hallelujah indeed.

But having learned how to arrange himself, is Richard fully equipped to organise other people? He now has to get to grips with the true art of delegating and to learn that *delegating is not a convenient device for continuing to interfere*.

> **Bernard:** So what do you think: minestrone or chicken soup? A choice of two main dishes or three? And do you want *me* to advertise for the new kitchen porter?
> **Richard:** That's up to you.
> **Bernard:** Yes, but as you always change my decisions, I thought I'd ask you first. *That* way, you can change them before I've made them, if you follow me.
> **Richard:** I only do your work because you can't even breathe in and out without asking me how to do it.
> **Bernard:** Yes, well, you keep interfering, you keep delegating jobs to me and then taking them back. I can never discuss anything with you and then you blow me up when it goes wrong.
> **Richard:** Aagh!

Richard consults St Peter.

> **Richard:** He's made me ill again.
> **St Peter:** You've made yourself ill again. Bernard's absolutely right. And if you don't pull your socks up I'm going to recall you to the after-life on a permanent basis. You've learned to organise yourself. Now learn to organise other people. You must learn to **delegate**.
> **Richard:** But I *do* delegate. I left Ginnie to manage my bring-forward files.

St Peter: It's her job anyway, that's secretarial work. I'm talking about you delegating part of your job.

Richard: Part of *my* job?

St Peter: Well, that's what delegation is, isn't it? Giving your subordinates the authority to decide, and without consulting you. Now, there are two barriers you've got to get through. The first one is that you have to give up doing some jobs that you like doing. There's a technical phrase for this: it's called growing up. Then you have to get over your fear of losing control.

Richard: But if my subordinates get it wrong, then I'll have to take the rap.

St Peter: Of course. Because it's part of *your* job you've delegated. You can delegate tasks and authority – you cannot delegate accountability.

Richard: It's still my job, although someone else is doing it?

St Peter: Yes. Your boss gets blamed for your mistakes and praised for your successes . . .

Richard: Well?

St Peter: So he'll understand if your subordinates make a few mistakes when work is first delegated to them, but he'll be pleased that you've delegated it because that'll mean you'll have more time for more important things.

Richard: It's such a risk.

St Peter: Of course it is, but with proper planning and training you can *limit* risk. Now first of all get it clear in your mind which task to delegate. Then ask yourself who is the person who can handle it, and then how long will it take him or her to learn to handle it. You can't delegate a new job without **proper training**. It's not fair on them and it'll only

You can't delegate a new job without proper training

involve you in more work later on. It takes time for a person to learn and to gain confidence. You've got to teach them, and you've got to make a training plan so that they know exactly when they're going to have to take full responsibility for the job. For example, what about that wretched letter to Mr Johnson?

Richard: Yes. I've got to do something about that. We open at the Royal Victoria Hall in seven weeks.

St Peter: Well, don't try to do it yourself. Delegate it to the District Manager.

Richard: Bernard?

St Peter: Well, why not? That's what he's there for.

Richard: What if it goes wrong?

St Peter: Look, there's nothing to worry about provided that you delegate it properly, provided that you . . .

Richard, all enthusiasm for this delegating business, has rushed back to Earth. It was, unquestionably, a good idea to delegate the job to Bernard, but it would have been even better if Richard had stayed long enough to hear what St Peter was going to say next. **Delegation is not the same thing as abdication** and Richard is about to make an elementary mistake . . .

Delegation is not the same as abdication

Richard: Bernard, I've got a proposal for you. I want *you* to take over the Royal Victoria Hall job.
Bernard: How do you mean?
Richard: I'm delegating it to you. All of it. I'm putting you in charge. Just you.
Bernard: Me?
Richard: How can I make it any clearer? Organise the staff, buy light equipment – cutlery, crockery, whisks, the usual – set out all the documentation and

bookwork, organise the notices, health and safety, training, our policy statement – and make sure that they're adhered to. Any questions?

Bernard: But all this stuff you're handing over to me – you've never allowed me to do it before.

Richard: I know, that's been my mistake. I'm asking you to do it and you know how, don't you? Fine. Now it's all up to you. I want you to stand on your own feet – I don't want to hear another word about it until I see you there on the opening day. It's all yours, mate!

Inevitably, Richard is summoned back by St Peter.

Richard: What am I doing here now? Why don't you let me get on with it?

St Peter: Because there's something else you have to learn.

Richard: I decided which task, who did it, and by when they'd be ready. He doesn't need any more help or training, he's already trained, so he's ready, right? And I briefed him.

St Peter: Yes, but . . .

Richard: Shut up! I informed others. I got it *all* right. So what have you got me up here again for? I can't spend time hanging around in Heaven when I've got important things to do down there.

St Peter: Would you care to look into the future?

Richard looks – apprehensively . . .

Richard: Ah, Bernard, come on in, come and sit down. Well now, how's it all going at the Victoria Hall?

Bernard: OK. But I think you ought to know that as you left it to me, I've played safe.

Richard: How do you mean, played safe?

Bernard: Well, the unions wanted a special deal for overtime.

Richard: Why didn't you tell me?

Bernard: You didn't ask. You said it was all up to me. So I thought . . . I'll have to give them what they're asking for.

Richard: My God. Is *this* the budget? It's a certain loss-maker. I could get the sack for this.

Bernard: You said you didn't want to be bothered.

Richard: But . . . but . . .

Richard demands an explanation from St Peter.

Richard: But I delegated it to Bernard. I gave him the job and left him to do it.

St Peter: Well, you gave him the authority to do the job, yes, but that doesn't mean you can just walk away from it.

Richard: You're confusing me. Leave him alone to do the job, but don't just walk away.

St Peter: Let's find an everyday example. Take your son, Darren.

Richard: Darren?

St Peter: Yes, Darren. Now, when you taught him to swim, you didn't just go home and leave him to it, did you? You got out of the pool, sure, but kept an eye on him in case of trouble, and as he became a stronger swimmer, so you needed to watch him less. Well, it's the same with delegation. You take your hands off but you keep your eyes open. So, be available to give advice in case you are needed, and monitor progress, check up on key points.

And it works. Bernard did not, actually, commit himself . . .

> **Bernard:** . . . But then I thought I'd better check with you.
> **Richard:** You mean – it's not too late?
> **Bernard:** No.
> **Richard:** Oh, Bernard. Thank you, thank you, thank you, thank you . . .

So Richard has realised that one of the essential components in delegating is a proper degree of **continued involvement**. Of course you follow Heavenly principles: make sure you know exactly what it is you are delegating, to whom the tasks are going, that they are capable of handling them, and that all the people concerned should know who is now doing that particular job. But it is absolutely essential to remember that the person who delegates a task cannot simply wash his hands of it. It is a balance which the good manager, like the good parent, will get right. Once you get it right, you will come home in the evenings and cope as easily as Richard does now!

Richard, at last with time for his family, has succeeded in mending his son's toy train.

> **Darren:** Daddy, it's super!
> **Richard:** Well, you go and get your face scrubbed. We're going to the pictures.
> **Darren:** Great!
> **Cathy:** What about your work?
> **Richard:** Work? Oh . . . *work*. I do that at the office now.

Golden rules

1 There is always time for planning.
2 Time is a budget item.
3 Divide your tasks into Active and Reactive.
4 The urgent is not the same as the important.
5 Schedule your time according to what's important.
6 Use 'to do' lists.
7 When you delegate you do not delegate accountability.
8 Delegation is not abdication.

3 The unorganised manager – Lamentations

The organised manager will, as we have seen, have learned about priorities, objectives, active and reactive tasks and the difference between the urgent and important. He will schedule time, make a 'to do' list, delegate sensibly and keep a healthy involvement which falls short of interference. In short, 'What am I here for?' will not be an unanswered question. *But*, getting yourself sorted out is only one part of the equation. How good are you at **getting your staff to ask themselves 'what am I here for?'** – and receiving the correct answer.

Getting yourself sorted out
is only one part of the equation

Remember they need the same degree of confidence and certainty in what they are doing as you do, and if they are falling down in the job the fault lies not in their stars but in their boss.

We left Richard Lewis in a state of grace. Let's follow his next steps, with the help of St Peter, who as we find him is giving an interview to a local reporter.

> **St Peter:** The *Celestial Times* colour supplement? Well, I don't talk to the Press much, I'm afraid . . .
> **Reporter:** If you could spare us a few moments, your Saintliness, we'd be very grateful. It's for a new series we're contemplating . . . 'A Day in the After-Life'.
> **St Peter:** I see, very well, do sit down. So you want to give people some idea of my job here as Gate Keeper?
> **Reporter:** Exactly.
> **St Peter:** Yes, well . . . I'm a kind of glorified immigration officer really . . .
> **Reporter:** Keeping all the rotters out?
> **St Peter:** The rotters, the cads, the bad hats. It's my job to weed out the black sheep – it's pretty straightforward really.
> **Reporter:** But you must get borderline cases from time to time – grey sheep as it were . . . when you have to exercise your powers of discretion.
> **St Peter:** Only very occasionally we get the odd mis-routing – there was a chap recently, should have gone to you-know-where, but the truth is he was a technical sinner not a baddie, so I decided to stretch a point and sent him back down again to try and teach him where he'd gone wrong. What was his name? Lucan . . . Lupin . . . not Lucifer but a bit like that . . . Luther? Lewis! Richard Lewis! Cor – if

ever there was an Unorganised Manager . . . Never sorted out his priorities – couldn't delegate to save his life – never had the time to do anything properly. In the end, of course, he snapped. Gave himself an early coronary. So anyway, yes, I decided to give Lewis a second chance. I explained to him – calmly and with great patience – that what he'd got to do was to *plan* his time . . . to work out his priorities by distinguishing between those tasks that were urgent and those that were important, and organise his time accordingly by allowing time for both Active and Reactive tasks. Do get that in, will you? Took a little time, of course, but eventually he got it and now he's one of the most organised managers on earth.

St Peter touches a button and they gaze down on the reformed Richard Lewis . . . He is in full control as he instructs his assistant Ginnie.

> **Richard:** There we are, Ginnie. That's the morning's correspondence. Now, 9.25 . . . my diary says . . . yes, ring Philip Tessler at BT. Well, he shouldn't present any problems. Ah, Mr Tessler? Richard Lewis at Parker and Gibbs Catering – we spoke yesterday . . .
> **Reporter:** Amazing. He's a different man.
> **St Peter:** Yes, I'm rather proud of it actually. Yes, I think you can take it from me, Richard Lewis is one Earthly executive we *will* be seeing up here. Now, tea . . . coffee . . . nectar?
> **Reporter:** Nectar, please – very dry.

They both lose interest in the TV which has moved to Lewis's District Managers. Barbara is planning a menu; Bernard is on the phone, harassed.

Bernard: Martin? Bernard here. How much are they asking? Just for an extra two-hour shift? I suppose we can *just* afford it . . . can we? Er . . . OK then, Martin, I imagine that as long as we keep our heads above water that'll be OK. 'Bye.

Barbara: Problems, Bernard?

Bernard: Er . . . I don't think so, Barbara. It's a bit difficult to tell, isn't it?

Barbara: Listen, Bernard – you've been in this job much longer than me – what do you think about this new menu for the canteen at Dibley's Ball-Bearings?

Bernard: Crunchy nut salad . . . what's tortelli?

Barbara: Pasta stuffed with spinach and cheese. Spinach is full of iron, you know.

Bernard: Mmm . . . you don't think bangers and mash would be a bit more . . .

Barbara: Oh Bernard! Sausages are full of preservatives, pork takes longer to digest than any other meat, and potatoes are 90 per cent water.

Tony breezes into the office.

Tony: Morning all! Morning Ginnie!

Ginnie: Nice to see *you*! You're working today, are you?

Tony: It's Tuesday.

Ginnie disappears into Richard's office.

Bernard: I thought Tuesday was golf. Or is that just Monday, Wednesday, Thursday and Friday?

Tony: No, Friday's gloating about my profits. How are yours, by the way? And Barbara, everyone's favourite. Come on love, give us a song . . .

Barbara: I'm tired, Tony, sorry. I was up half the night doing that stupid report.

Tony: Half the night!

Bernard: Report? What report?

Tony: I did mine when I came in this morning. Look, two pages, twenty minutes.

Barbara: Is that it?

Bernard: What *are* you talking about?

Barbara: The report on Projected Sales for the next quarter. He asked for it at the last meeting, remember?

Bernard: But . . . he didn't want that *today* surely . . .

Ginnie pops back.

Ginnie: Nine thirty, Mr Lewis will see you now.

They troop into Richard's office, Bernard anything but happy.

Richard: Right! That deals with that then, so let's move on to the Projected Sales reports I asked for last time . . .

Barbara and Tony hand theirs across.

Richard: Thank you very much, that's . . . what the hell's this?

Barbara: Well it's . . . the report . . .

Richard: I wanted a résumé, not *War and Peace*.

Barbara: Well, you never said how long you . . .

Richard: Oh Barbara, really!

Barbara: I was up till one putting that together.

Richard: I can believe it! It's a wonder your typewriter didn't get a hernia. I'm sorry, Barbara, time's a budget item with me these days, I can't wade through all this – just summarise it. Two pages is enough. Here, look. Like Tony's. *He* knew what I wanted.

Tony: Lucky guess really.

Richard: Sorry Tony? Bernard, I don't seem to have yours here . . .

Bernard: I'm afraid I haven't done it yet, Mr Lewis.

Richard: Haven't done it yet? But I *told* you I wanted it today.

Bernard: No you didn't. You just said you wanted it as soon as possible. And so far I'm afraid it *hasn't* been possible.

Richard: Oh dear, oh dear, oh dear!

Bernard: I'll try and get round to it first thing in the morning.

Richard: Well do, will you. This is putting *my* system right out of gear. Now look, I'll get straight to the point, everyone. A lot of things simply aren't good enough. I couldn't believe last month's figures when they came in. I mean, look at them – just look at them!

He waves a sheet of paper in the air. The others try and catch a glimpse but Richard has slapped them face down on the desk.

Richard: Well, I think they speak for themselves, don't they? And *one* of you I'm *particularly* disappointed in at the moment. I won't name any names, because I don't think it's right to embarrass her in front of others. But in general, there's a lot of room for improvement all round. Except Tony. Good work! So, for God's sake buck your ideas up. Now then.

He distributes some pamphlets.

Richard: That new vending machine I told you about last time. Here's the literature on it, and I want a big

autumn push on this one, it's a high profit item for us.
Tony: How many orders are you hoping for . . .
ideally?
Richard: As many as you can get.
Tony: Ah . . . I've got you.
Bernard: And *when* do you expect them in by?
Richard: As soon as possible. I mean, for goodness'
sake, use some comon sense, all of you. Do I have to
spell *everything* out?

Richard has opened the door to the outer office and all
three start to leave. He keeps Barbara behind.

> **Richard:** Now look, Barbara, I know you haven't
> been in the job as long as the other two, but really
> . . . you've got to do better than this, I'm afraid. You
> know what I'm talking about, don't you?
> **Barbara:** Oh . . . er . . . yes, of course, Mr Lewis.
> **Richard:** People just aren't happy with the type of
> food you're serving, Barbara.
> **Barbara:** But . . . Oh, I see . . . right, Mr Lewis.
> **Richard:** These people need something satisfying.
> You will try to do something about it, OK?
> **Barbara:** Yes, of course, I understand, Mr Lewis.
> **Richard:** Well, off you go then – and remember, it's
> my head that's on the chopping block, so pull your
> socks up, right?
> **Barbara:** I'll get down to it immediately.

Richard closes the door behind Barbara with a sigh and
a bang. The phone rings. He answers it.

> **Richard:** Richard Lewis. Oh, yes, sir! Yes, I've seen
> the figures. I've just been talking to them about it
> . . . Yes sir, I've told them exactly what's wrong, but
> they just don't seem able to . . . Yes, I realise it's not

good enough but what can you do when you've got idiots working for you? . . . What sir? No, I wasn't asking *you*, I was . . . hallo?

The phone is dead.

> **Richard:** Damn! Oh yes, that's really great! I get the blame for those hopeless, fat-headed morons. I'll tell 'em. Next time I'll really tell 'em.

Meanwhile, back in Heaven . . .

> **Reporter:** And what first interested you in gate-keeping, your Saintliness?
> **St Peter:** Do you know the story about the keys? It's quite a long one but you might be able to make something of it . . . you see there was this rock . . .

Not before time the reporter catches a glimpse of the TV. Richard is writhing on the floor.

> **Reporter:** Is he supposed to be doing that? I mean, is it a new management technique or something?
> **St Peter:** I think he's having another . . . excuse me . . . won't be a moment!

Richard has collapsed at his desk and is sobbing broken-heartedly. The door of a filing cabinet opens and St Peter steps out as if from a lift.

> **Richard:** Oh my God!
> **St Peter:** No, only his Personnel Manager I'm afraid. Are you all right?
> **Richard:** Yes . . . no! It just isn't fair. They don't *listen* to me and I get the blame. I mean, I keep on telling them but . . .
> **St Peter:** Keep it short . . . I'm doing an interview.
> **Richard:** It's a long story . . .

St Peter: Yes, but is it *urgent* or is it *important*?
Richard: What? Oh . . . er . . . both.
St Peter: You'd better come up . . . you can tell me on the way.

In Heaven the reporter nibbles her biscuit in the fore-ground as St Peter and Richard emerge from the lift. Richard has obviously been complaining bitterly.

Richard: . . . and I *always* get the blame. I'll be back in Intensive Care again at this rate, you mark my words. If you could see what a shambles they make of everything I ask them to do.
St Peter: May I introduce Miss Angela Cherabin . . . may I introduce Mr Richard Lewis? You may recall that Mr Lewis was, albeit briefly, an organised manager.
Reporter: Amazing!
Richard: I am organised – I did everything you said – planned, got my priorities right, delegated. It's not me that's the problem, it's *them*.
Reporter: The Powers of Darkness?
Richard: Yes! My District Managers. *Exactly*! They're useless. They don't know what they're supposed to be doing. Barbara hasn't the first idea. Bernard's a complete waste of space and Tony . . . well, Tony's quite good actually.
St Peter: Yes. This will take a few minutes.
Reporter: Oh that's all right – it's all good copy.
St Peter: Right. Now tell us about Barbara.
Richard: I always took her for such a bright young lady, that's the tragedy of it. First class reports when she was a Unit Manager – wonderful boardroom lunches – but since we moved her up she's been a disaster.

St Peter: Oh?

Richard: I put her in charge of some of our best contracts. After three months, sales were on the slide – the number of customers lunching on-site had started to drop like a stone.

St Peter: She's losing you money.

Richard: It's only a matter of time. She's over budget on food costs in most of her areas. And these are our bread and butter contracts. A child of five could manage them. Heaven knows what she gets up to when she goes round those canteens.

St Peter: Yes, we do, so why don't you take a look, Mr Lewis? You never know, you might learn something. Miracles have been known to happen. Let's have a look at a typical moment from Barbara's working day.

He touches a control button and the screen shows Barbara in the foreground talking to the Catering Manager. Behind them two burly workers in overalls unload their trays and sit at a table. Barbara finishes writing.

Barbara: Right then, after the quiche, I thought a nice passion-fruit sorbet in a little glass . . .

Catering Manager: We've only got dishes or tumblers.

Barbara: That's all right. I'll find the money for them from somewhere . . . Now then . . .

Behind her the two men regard their meals with suspicion. They pass the plates – which bear strange, tiny portions – one to the other to sniff.

Barbara: Any problems with the Summer Symphony?

Catering Manager: Well, the chicory and the wild

mushrooms are rather expensive, so there's not a lot
per customer.
Barbara: I know, it's shocking, isn't it? Still, at least
they're getting their zinc.

One of the men forks something up, takes a bite gingerly,
then pushes the plate away in distaste, and opens a bag
of crisps which he offers to his colleague.

Barbara: Next week we might go for a bit more
variety. I'm thinking of getting everyone to do a
Malaysian Rice Table . . .

There is a reaction in Heaven.

Richard: Malaysian Rice Table! Summer Symphony!
I told you she's an idiot.
St Peter: Why?
Richard: That was Dibley's Ball-Bearings! Those
lads can't do a decent day's work on a zinc sorbet!
Surely she must know that!
St Peter: Must she? Have you told her?
Richard: Of course I've told her. I've told her time
and time again to buck her ideas up. She's got to do a
better job than that.
St Peter: Yes, but have you ever told her exactly
what her job *is*?
Richard: Well, I shouldn't have to do that, should I?
St Peter: Shouldn't you?
Richard: Well, it's obvious, isn't it?
Reporter: Unfortunately not. If it was, she'd be
getting it right.
Richard: No . . . you don't understand what I'm on
about.
St Peter: Join the club. Now let's move on to
Bernard.

Richard: Bernard, don't talk to me about Bernard. Run a business? He couldn't run a bath! Do you know what he did yesterday morning?
St Peter: Yes, but why don't we watch an action replay?

He touches the button. They watch a worried Bernard talking to Ginnie.

Bernard: I don't suppose Richard has signed that renewal proposal for Ludgate's yet?
Ginnie: I think he's just reading it through now . . .
Bernard: Ah well, I'll come back later then, when he's . . .

At that moment Richard appears from his office clutching the proposal.

Richard: Bernard, what's *this*?
Bernard: Er . . . the renewal proposal for Ludgate's.
Richard: I can see that. You've agreed to pass on an extra three per cent discount! Do you realise what that'll do to us? Have you taken leave of your senses?
Bernard: Well, they *were* very insistent, Mr Lewis – in any case we can afford it . . . can't we?
Richard: We're not a public service, Bernard! Most of your units are only operating at two per cent profit as it is.
Bernard: Well, how much are they *supposed* to make?
Richard: A damned sight more than that. At this rate we'd be better off closing down the canteen and putting the money in a deposit account!
Bernard: Would we?

Richard looks helplessly at St Peter.

Richard: You see, that's what I have to put up with.

St Peter: Incomprehension you mean? Lack of understanding? People failing to read your mind – that sort of thing?

Richard: Exactly! And I'm right, aren't I? We're a business, not a public service.

St Peter: And certainly not a Secret Service.

Richard: Pardon?

Reporter: But have you ever told him what profit he should be making?

Richard: Yes! Of course I have. Every month I say to him this isn't good enough. Pull your socks up.

St Peter: It's lucky I have the patience of a saint. Now then – what about Tony?

Richard: Tony? He's not so bad – quite bright, knows the business, good profits, but he's lazy. He just does what's necessary and that's all you get.

St Peter: I wonder why. Let's see what he'll be doing at . . . 11.30 tomorrow morning.

The button is pressed. Tony is speaking to one of his Catering Managers in the car park.

Tony: These menus seem fine. Any other problems?

Manager: There's a hiccup over the new overtime rates, I don't know *how* we're going to . . .

Tony: That's OK – I've got a deal up my sleeve, I think, that will sort that one out – we can have a word with Bob about it tomorrow.

Manager: Oh, right – there's also the crisis over the meat deliveries . . .

Tony: I've looked into that. I've written it down – here – give this guy a ring and mention my name. I think he'll pull some strings. Nothing else?

Manager: No.

Tony: Right. There's another good day's work done

. . . and it's only a quarter to twelve. I've got an hour to kill before lunch.

Manager: Some of us have got work to do.

Tony: Lucky old you.

And in Heaven:

St Peter: Well, it's not good enough. Pull your socks up then.

Richard: How?

St Peter: Exactly! Well, let's start by analysing your problem.

Richard: *Their* problem, you mean.

Reporter: Oh that's funny . . . that's really funny! May I quote you on that? This stuff on Mr Lewis . . . it's wonderful. We do a 'Lost Sheep' every week.

St Peter: Now, about this problem of yours . . . there's Barbara who doesn't know what she's supposed to be doing, Bernard who doesn't know how well he's supposed to be doing it – and Tony who hasn't got *enough* to do.

Richard: Yes.

St Peter: And there's you who can organise yourself but who can't **organise other people**. Well, I suppose we'd better start right at the end?

Richard: I beg your pardon?

St Peter: Well, you have to have an end before you can have a beginning. See?

Golden rules

1 Rely on clarity, not clairvoyance.
2 Ask 'Am I in any way responsible?' before you start blaming others for mistakes.
3 Never use 'Pull your socks up'-type generalities.
4 Organising others isn't boring, it's sanity.
5 You can't function in the light if your colleagues are functioning in the dark.

4 The unorganised manager – Revelations

The last chapter dealt with some very common problems – those of a seemingly well-organised manager who failed to organise others. Make no mistake, in the vast majority of cases a disorganised staff, or staff member, is the boss's responsibility. There is no merit in a pep talk which amounts to 'I'm looking for an improvement from you'. Without detail – how, when, where, why and what – such exhortations are worse than useless.

Not all of us are lucky enough to have St Peter as a management guru, but Richard Lewis is. We'll continue the discussion . . .

> **Richard:** What do you mean, start at the end?
> **St Peter:** Oh, all right. Anyway, it's too late for that now. We'll have to start at the beginning. So you can organise yourself, but you can't organise other people. Right?
> **Richard:** Yes, but why can't they organise *themselves*?
> **St Peter:** It's your . . .
> **Richard:** I mean, they're just so hopeless and dim, why don't you get them up here and grill them too?
> **St Peter:** We don't grill up here. They look after that in the basement. As you'll probably soon discover. Unless, of course, you go to the *lower* basement.
> **Richard:** *Lower* basement?
> **St Peter:** Yes, the basement is for those who fail. The lower basement is for the failures who blame their failure on their subordinates. So let's look at your three District Managers, three people each

representing a particular failure of yours. First of all, let's look at Barbara who doesn't understand what she's supposed to be doing because you failed to tell her clearly what her responsibilities are. Then there's Bernard who doesn't know how well he's supposed to be doing because you failed to give standards of performance that he could measure his efforts by. And finally there's Tony who's wasting a lot of time because you haven't given him enough targets. Targets to keep him interested and develop his potential and get the best out of him. Three failures, therefore, to **clarify responsibilities**, to **set standards** and to **agree targets**.

Richard: But it's not my fault.

St Peter: Could you say that a little louder? I'm not sure they caught it down in the lower basement . . . Now, let's start with your first problem.

Richard: Barbara? No, *not* Barbara! *My* failure to clarify . . . Barbara's . . .

St Peter: The first thing you've got to do with your subordinates is to tell them what their job is.

Richard: They *know* that!

St Peter: Really?

Richard: Well, they're not missionaries, or tail gunners, are they? They're District Managers in a catering company.

St Peter: Tony and Bernard may have found out their job the hard way, but Barbara certainly doesn't know.

Lewis: Well, what does *she* think it is then?

St Peter: Why don't we find out?

He taps a couple of keys and the TV comes on. Barbara is sitting with a female friend . . .

> **Barbara:** You see – I'm what's called a District Manager.
> **Friend:** What does that involve?
> **Barbara:** Well, I'm a sort of ideas woman and advisor, primarily, to a series of canteens. My job is to use my knowledge and experience of catering to make sure the meals are exciting and varied enough – and above all nutritionally balanced, high protein, low carbohydrates, plenty of fibre and the key vitamins and minerals. Quite a challenge really.

There is a startled reaction in Heaven.

> **Richard:** I . . . I . . . I . . .
> **St Peter:** Well, do you agree with her description of the job?
> **Richard:** Gaaaa . . .
> **St Peter:** Well, how is she to find out from you what her job *is*? Tarot cards, reading the tea leaves in your empty cups, or extra-sensory perception? Wait a tick! I've had a brainwave! How about telling her? And when you do tell her, start at the beginning. Remember a useful little phrase, 'What am I here for?' Simple, isn't it? So what is Barbara there for, then?
> **Richard:** About another twenty-four hours if she doesn't buck . . .
> **St Peter:** Have you told her what her job is?
> **Richard:** A thousand times . . . I told her half an hour ago.
> **St Peter:** Did you? I think we should take a look at what you actually said, this time with subtitles for all those poor people who aren't telepathic.

The TV replays the scene:

> **Richard:** Now Barbara. I know you've not been in the job as long as the other two, but really you've got to do better than this, I'm afraid. You know what I'm talking about, don't you? I mean it's not as if you were totally new to the business.

And St Peter flashes up a subtitle: 'I'm talking about falling profits'.

> **Barbara:** No . . . er . . . yes, of course, Mr Lewis.

Subtitle: 'What are you talking about?'

> **Richard:** People just aren't happy with the type of food you're serving, Barbara.

Subtitle: 'Your meals are too ruddy exotic.'

> **Barbara:** But . . . Oh, I see . . . right, Mr Lewis.

Subtitle: 'My meals still aren't exciting enough.'

> **Richard:** These people need something . . . satisfying. So you *will* do something about it, OK?

Subtitle: 'Provide something more suited to canteens.'

> **Barbara:** Yes, of course. I understand, Mr Lewis.

Subtitle: 'I misunderstand, Mr Lewis.'

> **Richard:** . . . She didn't quite get my drift, did she?
> **St Peter:** Not totally, no. So you must define for her clearly what her **responsibilities** are. What are they?
> **Richard:** To see each of her catering units operates to the highest standard possible while balancing our clients' requirements against profitability with due regard to company policy.

St Peter: Good. Then you must make her responsibilities even clearer, by **defining key areas** where she is expected to get results.
Richard: Ah, that's not so easy.
St Peter: I thought it might not be. Let's put it another way. What are the principal areas in which your District Managers can cock things up?
Richard: Ha! Don't get me on to that one! . . . over-spending, complaints from customers, failing a public health inspection . . .
St Peter: Right, there's three for a start.
Richard: Three what?
St Peter: Three key areas where you can establish you need decent results: budget control, customer satisfaction and hygiene. Now do those define the job fully?
Richard: No . . . there's also profitability . . . new business . . .
St Peter: Two more key result areas. Now would you like to tell some of this to Barbara? Tomorrow . . . 9.30?
Richard: OK.

St Peter taps keys, and so, the scene in the office next morning is replayed:

Barbara: But I thought I was promoted because everyone was going on about my sense of originality. I thought you wanted the same approach.
Richard: Well, that's my fault for not making your new job clearer. That was great when you were a Unit Manager for a directors' boardroom, but it's not right now for works canteens. You see, your canteen takings have dropped by nearly twenty per cent over the last two months.

Barbara: Have they?

Richard: But . . . you should know that!

Barbara: Should I? I thought that if they were unhappy with . . .

Richard: It's one of your principal responsibilities. How many times have I told you . . . I . . . er, look. What I should have done is clarify what you're here for. I wrote this out . . .

Barbara: Oh!

Richard: Yes . . . then I've broken it up into parts. I'll be doing the same with Bernard and Tony, incidentally.

Barbara: Key areas . . .

Richard: Right. They're the make-or-break areas which comprise your job. I'd like to go through each of them with you now and then again in two weeks' time to hear any suggestions you may have.

Barbara: Oh right . . .

St Peter re-caps religiously:

St Peter: So the first lesson in organising your staff successfully is to . . .

1 Define their responsibilities. Tell them what they're there for. Then . . .
2 Establish the key areas in which the person doing that job must achieve results and . . .
3 Review them regularly to make sure your employee always has the same view of the job as you do.

Richard: Well, that all helped me with Barbara. But it doesn't solve Bernard's problem, does it? He knows what his responsibilities are, but he doesn't get decent results.

St Peter: But how do you expect Bernard to get decent results if you don't tell him which results are decent?
Richard: Come again?
St Peter: All right, we've dealt with *Responsibilities*; lesson two is *Standards*.

Lesson Two is Standards

Richard: Ah, I'm a stickler for standards!
St Peter: Are you?
Richard: Oh yes . . . every month I call him in and I say, 'Bernard, this still isn't good enough, pull your socks up!'
St Peter: How far? How far do you tell Bernard to pull his socks up? An inch? Three inches? A foot?
Richard: I don't understand.
St Peter: Well, it's not good enough is it? You're not doing your job properly. You've got to do better.
Richard: But how?

St Peter: By bucking your ideas up. By getting a grip on yourself. Above all, by pulling your socks up.
Richard: But *how*!??
St Peter: Exactly! All those phrases . . . useless! Woolly management at its worst . . . A substitute for thought and no help to *anyone*. Now, look . . . Every employee needs to be set **standards of achievement** below which he must not fall. These need to be visible, common to everyone in the same job, and fixed – a yardstick by which the employee can measure his activities for himself. If you don't give them a yardstick you get *this* . . .

The TV jumps to life. Bernard is talking to a workman who has just finished looking the kitchen over.

Workman: We're talking about a complete refit really. Replace cookers, install new deep-freeze units, streamline all work surfaces. You won't get it done cheaper than that, I promise you. Here's an estimate . . .
Bernard: My God! Will it really cost this much?
Workman: Listen, I'm doing you a favour.
Bernard: I have to be so careful, that's the trouble. I never know when my boss is suddenly going to bite my head off . . . still, I *think* we're making enough to cover it.

And in Heaven Richard is holding his head in his hands.

St Peter: You see? The poor man didn't *know* whether he could afford that contract or not. He's having to operate by guesswork.
Richard: Guesswork?
St Peter: Yes. You remember that report your staff handed in this morning.

The key is pressed.

> **Richard:** What the hell's this?
> **Barbara:** Well, it's . . . the report . . .
> **Richard:** I meant a summary – not *War and Peace*.
> Two pages is enough. Here, look at Tony's – he
> knew what I wanted.
> **St Peter:** If you only wanted two pages you should
> have told them. You could have said something like,
> 'I only want two pages'. It's not difficult.

And back to the office:

> **Richard:** Bernard, I don't seem to have yours here.
> **Bernard:** I'm afraid I haven't done it yet, Mr Lewis.
> **Richard:** Haven't done it? But I *told* you I wanted it
> today.
> **Bernard:** No you didn't. You just said you wanted it
> as soon as possible and so far, I'm afraid, it hasn't
> been possible.

St Peter continues the sermon:

> **St Peter:** If you wanted the report handed in by a
> certain day why didn't you say so? If you'd only set
> precise standards in the first place you wouldn't have
> caused all that confusion.
> **Richard:** What is a standard then?
> **St Peter:** A standard, quite simply, is a measurement
> imposed *by* you – on your staff – which tells them
> exactly what is expected of them. It enables your staff
> *themselves* to know how well they are doing their jobs,
> and keeps them up to the mark. It helps them.
> **Richard:** I follow the theory, but you can't actually
> set measurable standards in all jobs, can you?
> **St Peter:** If you think about it, you'll find you can.

Let us imagine you're a Sales Director. And . . . this is more difficult . . . let's imagine that you're an *effective* one.

The TV shows Richard as a Sales Director. He hands a sheet of paper to a new salesman.

Richard as Sales Director: Now these are the minimum standards we expect from our salesmen. No fewer than *ten* cold calls each month – all call reports filed within *seven* working days of a visit . . . and a minimum of *eighty* calls to be made per month to existing customers . . .

The lesson is absorbed.

Richard: Ah – I see! I'm laying down **precise quotas** so my staff can see at once if things aren't up to scratch.
St Peter: Right.
Richard: Ah . . . but Sales is easy!
St Peter: All right . . . you're a Production Manager.

St Peter hits a key. Richard is a Production Manager with a Print Supervisor. They are looking at booklet artwork.

Richard as Production Manager: Right. So, we've agreed on a maximum of sixteen and three-quarter per cent paper wastage, three hours' setting-up time, and four and a half hours' printing.

Another objection.

Richard: Well, all right . . . but Sales and Production are easy to quantify, but you can't have measurable standards for everything.
St Peter: You can. You'll find everything's

measurable in terms of one or more of these four
factors: QUALITY, QUANTITY, TIME, COST.
Richard: Everything? What about setting standards
for . . . clerical staff?
St Peter: Off you go.

And current performance will probably be well below 100%.
No staff member can be consistently perfect . . .

St Peter taps his keys and miraculously Richard is now
in charge of clerical staff.

> **Richard as Clerical Supervisor:** Er . . . eighty
> invoices to be processed per day . . . No more than

three per cent error rate . . . filing, no more than
three days behind . . .

Joy in Heaven.

> **Richard:** I did it!
> **St Peter:** Yes. So, do you think you can now sort out
> Bernard's problems? He knows what he's supposed
> to be doing but . . .
> **Richard:** . . . doesn't know how well he should be
> doing it. Well, I'll tell him.
> **St Peter:** What will you tell him?
> **Richard:** To undertake a quantity survey to show
> that 100 per cent of the workforce take meals in
> canteens, no complaints at all . . .
> **St Peter:** You've got to be realistic! Your staff are
> human beings. Standards must be achievable. Now,
> do it properly . . . tomorrow afternoon.

Tomorrow afternoon.

> **Richard:** So, in future, Bernard, we will budget a
> minimum of five per cent income per unit, on each
> contract. If you, or Barbara or Tony, fall below that
> figure I'll want to know the reason why.
> **Bernard:** Five per cent. Right, Mr Lewis.
> **Richard:** Well, the ball's in your court. No . . . wait
> . . . there's something . . . Yes. Standards in your
> other key result areas.
> **Bernard:** I beg your pardon?
> **Richard:** Of course, your attention to profitability
> musn't make you forget your other areas of
> responsibility. I am setting a rule that I don't want
> more than two justifiable complaints a year from any
> of your clients: and two six-month surveys to show at
> least eighty-five per cent of the workforce take their

meals in the canteen. And, er . . . monthly reports from you on hygiene and new business. OK?
Bernard: OK. Yes. That's a great help, Mr Lewis, thank you.
Richard: Not at all.

Richard returns to Heaven with some complacency.

Richard: All right?
St Peter: Eventually, yes. Now he knows what he's got to do and he can tell if he's done it.
Richard: But suppose . . . he hasn't done it?
St Peter: Then you've given both of yourselves an early warning system, haven't you? So if the results start falling below standard, you can start resolving the shortfalls immediately. But I guarantee you that when clearly measurable standards are set, employees will start resolving the shortfall themselves. Because they know where they stand. Watch Bernard . . .

They watch Bernard.

Workman: We're talking about a complete refit really . . . replace cookers . . .
Bernard: It won't do, I'm afraid.
Workman: You won't get it done cheaper than that, I promise you.
Bernard: We'll stick with the existing cookers – they've still got a few years of life in them. I can't go above £20,000.
Workman: £20,000. Well . . . with a cheaper worktop range . . . mm . . . we might just be able to accommodate you . . .

St Peter gives his sermon.

St Peter: So, the second lesson of successful staff management is:

1 Set standards.
2 Ensure that they can be measured by the manager *and* the employee and . . .
3 Discuss and resolve any shortfalls without delay.

Richard: I see! OK, I've got it. Well, thanks very much.

St Peter: Happy?

Richard: Absolutely, yes . . .

St Peter: Nothing else? What about . . . Tony?

Richard: Tony? No problem. He's very good . . . bit lazy, which gets to the others now and again. I wish I could get two more like him.

St Peter: You might get one *less* like him. Tony should have left you long ago.

Richard: What? But he gets a good salary. Lots of time off, his work's good, what more does he want?

St Peter: To use your horrible jargon – motivation.

Richard: Motivation?

St Peter: Let's talk about **Targets**. You see, Tony is frustrated because he's not being given enough work to tax his considerable talents. It's like asking Shostakovich to write radio jingles. The result is his heart's not in the job: and the others all resent him because they feel he's not really involved. It's not good for staff relations, and it's not good for the company.

Richard: But I can't sack him, he's the best I've got. I know . . . I'll *threaten* to sack him!

St Peter: You know, sometimes I find it quite hard,

loving you. No, Tony needs . . . ugh . . .
motivation.

Richard: Ah ha! So, in Tony's case I just tell him his
standards are higher than everyone else's.

St Peter: No, no, no. You're not thinking. *Standards*
have to be the same for all three of your managers or
they're not standards, are they? A standard is the
minimum requirement for the job. The 'pass' mark,
if you like. If he falls below it, our employee will be
failing to do his job. *Targets* are something the
forward-thinking manager will **agree** with individual
people, over and above the required standards,
according to their different capabilities. The 'credits'
they can go for, if you like.

Richard: You mean . . . Standards are *imposed* –
they're kind of fixed laws that everyone has to obey,
but Targets are *agreed*, individually with each
employee.

St Peter: That's very good. Yes, the Standards say,
'This is wht you *must* achieve'. Targets tell you what
it would be *desirable* to achieve. Now, give me some
examples of targets you might agree with individuals?

Richard: Well . . . say, trim a day off a particular
schedule, or get the monthly sales figures up another
one or two per cent above the standard.

St Peter: Right! This is what you'll say to Tony on
Wednesday morning.

And on to Wednesday morning:

Richard: So, how about it, Tony – how far do you
think you can get your income up in the next two or
three months?

Tony: Well, I suppose if I'm being honest, I could
manage seven per cent . . .

Richard: I think *you* could manage eight.

Tony: But, look . . . why should my target be eight when Bernard's is six, and Barbara's is only five?

Richard: Because they're struggling to achieve those figures, but they're no challenge to you. And as you go on to other roles in the company you'll need a record of high performance. So . . . eight per cent?

Tony: . . . no problem.

St Peter's sermon:

> **St Peter:** So, you see:
>
> 1 Targets are designed to stretch people and to harness their individual capabilities.
> 2 Targets are agreed between the manager and the individual and are often project-based; standards are common and imposed, targets are individual and agreed.
> 3 Standards are on-going, targets are often short-term. But a target, like a standard, will have agreed review criteria and use the same type of measures – quality, quantity, cost and time.
>
> Got it?
>
> **Richard:** Yes, I have. Can I go now?
>
> **St Peter:** No, no, wait. I want to show you what happens at your meeting with the District Managers in two months' time.

The office comes on to the screen. The District Managers are waiting impatiently: Bernard gazing through the window, Tony humming, Barbara checking through some papers.

> **Richard:** Hey! I'm not there.

St Peter: No.

Richard: Where am I?

St Peter: You're late. Watch.

Bernard: It's not like him to be late.

Barbara: Doesn't matter. Well, we all know how we're doing anyway.

Bernard: Yes – he can't moan at me. Six per cent, bang on.

Barbara: And I only missed the five per cent by a whisker. Another couple of weeks and I think I'll have got back all the 'nice-hot-meal' brigade.

Tony: Where the hell is he? I've got work to do.

Heaven rejoices.

St Peter: Congratulations. Now, one more time. Can I hear the lessons?

Richard: The first lesson. If a manager is to organise his staff successfully he must define their responsibilities. The second lesson is to set standards. The third lesson is to agree targets with each employee individually. And that is the end of the lessons.

St Peter: Amen, Hallelujah!

Golden rules

1 What am I here for? You and your colleagues must know the answer.
2 Define key areas of a job and let the person doing it know.
3 Set standards of achievement and remember they are not variable.
4 Set targets of performance and remember they are variable.
5 Agree targets with your employees.

5 Paperchase

Between 1955 and 1959 Marks and Spencer's profit turnover shot up from eight per cent to eleven per cent. It was the result of the Chairman's crusade to get rid of unnecessary paperwork. In fact they got rid of 26 million pieces of paper a year, weighing 120 tons. And they were already famous as an efficient company before the Chairman began his crusade.

And they made an interesting discovery. Excessive paperwork wasn't just wasteful and inefficient in itself: it actually created inefficiency. More paper creates more work and more work creates more paper. Paper distracts people. It delays them: they can't find important documents because they're smothered by unimportant ones.

Getting rid of paper raises morale and frees people to talk to colleagues, customers and supporters. It lets them use their memory and their common sense and their ideas instead of just following instructions and filling in forms. It shows you trust them.

Every organisation in the modern world knows it has a paper problem, and if we ever thought the computer was going to solve it we know better by now. It can only be solved by people. Top management obviously has the ultimate responsibility, but the real answer lies with every user of paper. It's an attitude of mind. It needs almost a religious conversion. It means avoiding using paper, avoiding asking for paper, and getting rid of every piece of paper you don't genuinely need. The Marks and Spencer motto was 'If in doubt, throw it out'.

Is this one of your mottos? It certainly wasn't Delia Dalton's. Delia's job is in Central Services, a department in a large company. Her office is one mass of folders, files, printouts, memos, circulars – they have invaded her desk, chairs, much of the floor, the window sill, hidden the telephone . . . Familiar? Delia's boss, Graham Benson, is soon to be succeeded by Joanna North. We'll follow Joanna as she makes her first, unexpected, visit to Delia's office. Delia, as usual, is searching phlegmatically for some information she needs . . .

> **Delia:** Come in.
> **Joanna:** Graham Benson suggested . . .
> **Delia:** Oh yes. Trainee attachment or something, wasn't it?
> **Joanna:** No. Actually I'm your new . . .
> **Delia:** Oh, take a seat. The phone . . . hello, Delia Dalton, Central Services . . . Oh, yes, Harry.

Joanna takes a chair. She moves the papers off it on to the floor and sits down.

Delia: You said you'd let me have the monthly figures. Did you? Oh well, I'll have another look. 'Bye.

Delia rings off and starts looking through the papers on her desk.

Delia: Sorry. He's already sent them apparently . . .

She goes on looking and picks up a brochure.

Delia: Have you ever been to an office equipment exhibition? Looks very interesting anyway.

She puts it back under other papers.

Delia: You'll find us a jolly efficient lot here.
Joanna: I'm actually not a trainee . . .

But the phone rings again and Delia picks it up.

Delia: Delia Dalton, Central Services . . . Ah, yes. Thanks for ringing back. I wasn't happy with your last invoice . . . Yes, but you only came three times. Hold on. I was looking at it last Tuesday and I had it here right in front of me then. Look. I can't put my hand on it at the moment. I'll have to call you back. OK, thanks. 'Bye. Sorry about that. You have to watch maintenance contracts like a hawk. Right now, where were we?
Joanna: 'A jolly efficient lot.'
Delia: That's right. Well, er . . . what is your name?
Joanna: Joanna North.
Delia: Now then, Joanna North. Has anyone told you how Central Services is actually organised?

Joanna: No.

Delia: No, well, there's Office Services. We've got Staff Services, we've got Building Services and we've got Communication Services. Now Office Services . . . do you know, I don't know why I'm telling you all this. I wrote a note on this last year. I'll just get it for you. Excuse me, thank you . . . I think it must be somewhere in this pile.

Joanna: What's all that?

Delia: This is last year's organisational development project. You know, reports, memos, background reading and the coursework.

Joanna: What was the project?

Delia: It was 'The Paperless Office'. Very, very useful, actually.

There is a knock at the door. One of the supervisors, Peter, comes in.

Delia: Come in. Yes, what is it, Peter?

Peter: Oh, sorry. It's about this telephone requisition form. I was wondering if you can give me a hand? I haven't done one before.

Delia: What is it?

Peter: It's boxes four to nine.

Delia: Yes. Well, those references are in the file.

Peter: Have you got it?

Delia: Yes . . . I had it somewhere . . . look, why don't you give that to me and I'll do it later.

Peter: Oh, thanks. By the way, I went to that presentation and it wasn't very relevant.

Delia: Please don't tell me now. Send me a copy of your report, would you?

Peter: Right.

Delia: Thank you.

He leaves his papers on Delia's desk and goes out. Delia finds the notes she is looking for and hands them to Joanna.

Joanna: Thank you. May I ask you a question?
Delia: Of course.
Joanna: Don't you think there's rather a lot of paper in this office?
Delia: Of course there is. That's what work is all about.
Joanna: Really? You see, I thought it was about people, not paper.
Delia: No, it isn't.
Joanna: But don't things get lost?
Delia: What things?
Joanna: Well, Harry's monthly figures. The maintenance invoice.
Delia: Oh, those things. No, no, I'll find them in due course. I know where everything is. It may take a bit of time, but it works. Nothing is ever lost.
Joanna: But some things are never found?
Delia: Well, only a few.
Joanna: But if it was filed?
Delia: Well, you see, if it was filed I'd definitely lose it. This way it's all where I can put my hand on it.
Joanna: Suppose you were ill?
Delia: I'm never ill.
Joanna: But suppose you were ill, and someone else had to do your job?
Delia: Yes, but I'm never ill, am I, Joanna? You'll learn that we all have different styles and this is my style, you see.

The phone rings and Delia picks it up.

Delia: Delia Dalton, Central Services. Yes, but I'm

still waiting for Harry's figures . . . Yes, I know he does . . . Yes, well, I'll have another look and get back to you.

The caller has rung off. Delia starts burrowing.

Delia: Honestly. The impatience of some people. Got to find . . .

She comes across the exhibition brochure again and leafs through it.

Delia: Do you think I should go to this office equipment exhibition?
Joanna: It ended three weeks ago.
Delia: Did it? Oh yes, you're right. Well back it goes.

She puts it back on the desk.

Joanna: Why are you keeping it?
Delia: Well, I don't want to throw it away, do I?
Joanna: Why not?
Delia: Well you never . . . Joanna North, may I say I know you are a trainee and you're supposed to ask questions, but you are asking rather a lot of them. You'll find the answers . . . in due course I hope. Ah, you see, Harry's monthly figures.

A memo is caught under the paper clip. She reads it.

Delia: Mmm. Never saw this before. It's not the 17th, is it?
Joanna: Yes.
Delia: Well, you'd better get along, young lady, because the new Head of Department's coming round today. Joanna North. *Joanna North*. That's funny. That's the same name as you. You're not

Joanna North, are you?

Joanna: Yes I am.

Delia: Well you might have said.

Joanna: Yes. I might.

Delia: Well, Joanna North. Are you happy with everything?

Joanna: No, I'm not.

Delia: Oh. What aren't you happy with?

Joanna: Guess.

Delia: The organisation? The layout? Furnishing? Weather? . . . Me?

Joanna: Yes.

Delia: Why?

Joanna: In your file it says you are intelligent, loyal, conscientious and hard-working. But hardly anything ever seems to get done.

Delia: Hang on. You've been reading my annual appraisals, haven't you?

Joanna: Yes. Now why do you think it says that?

Delia: I don't know.

Joanna: Any clues? Sort of, lying around the office? Paper?

Delia: What do you mean?

Joanna: You are shackled by a great chain of paper.

Delia: I am not.

Joanna: Yes you are. You couldn't find Harry's monthly returns or the maintenance invoice. You made Peter leave his papers instead of just giving him a verbal answer.

Delia: No, you've got it all . . .

Joanna: You wanted a copy of his report instead of just telling you about the presentation.

Delia: You've got it all wrong!

Joanna: You waste ages looking for things. You have

to make all your phone calls twice. You get distracted by out-of-date exhibition brochures. You have to work on the floor because there's no room on your desk . . .
Delia: Please!
Joanna: You're a paper-slave. Aren't you?
Delia: No. I am not. I'm sorry but this is my office. This is the way I want it. It suits me. It stimulates my imagination. It inflames my creative psyche.

Joanna points to a graph on Delia's desk.

Joanna: What is this?
Delia: It's a graph.
Joanna: I know that. What kind of graph is that?
Delia: Well it shows actuals against budgets, doesn't it?
Joanna: Creative psyche? This is trainee's work.
Delia: I know that. I'm doing it as a favour for Mr Hardcastle. He's very appreciative.

Joanna suddenly leans over Delia. Her voice has become hard and menacing.

Joanna: Are you sure it isn't just a hobby. Paper-slaves do things to escape. Because they are so scared. They are scared of all those letters, those faxes, those memos, those reports. They keep coming. And coming . . . And coming. Contracts. Invoices. Completion certificates. They pin you down. You can't move. You can't breathe and you suffocate . . . Delia Dalton. What are you?
Delia: Sacked.
Joanna: No. What's your job?
Delia: Oh, Central Services Co-ordinator.
Joanna: Co-ordinator. Exactly. You're in the driving seat.

Delia: Yes, I am.

Joanna: But you're not driving, are you? You're letting all this paper drive you. You're using activity as a substitute for achievement. You should be an engine, but you're just a wheel.

Delia: A big wheel?

Joanna: No. A little wheel. A little tiny cog. And all this paper that you are using as a lifebelt is actually a millstone and that is why you are sinking.

Delia: I am not sinking.

Joanna: Yes you are. But you can escape. What you need is a plan.

Delia: Have you got one?

Joanna: Yes. Listen very carefully. There are only four kinds of paper in this office. And those are:

1 Action papers – things you have to do.
2 Information – papers you have to read.
3 Papers which have to be kept. And . . .
4 JUNK.

A short while later . . .

Joanna: Good. Let's start with the **junk**. The out-of-date catalogue is an excellent beginning.
Delia: No, I can't.
Joanna: Why not?
Delia: Well . . . it . . . it cost a lot of money. It might be quite interesting.
Joanna: Tear it in half!
Delia: NO! I can't!
Joanna: Yes, do it. Be strong. Just think, no more lost memos, time to think. Time to plan. Organise. Talk to people. Meet your suppliers.
Delia: . . . I can't.

Joanna taps on the folder containing Delia's annual report. She quotes:

Joanna: 'Loyal, conscientious, hard-working. But hardly anything ever seems to get done.'
Delia: All right, all right . . . There!
Joanna: That wasn't very difficult, was it?
Delia: It might have had something important in it.
Joanna: The rule is that *everything gets thrown away unless there's a very good reason why it shouldn't.* What about those catalogues?
Delia: Well, there was something in one of them.
Joanna: Well, just tear out the relevant page and junk the rest. Now what about these reports?

Delia: Oh yes, we decided against those.

Joanna: Junk.

Delia: These are some job application forms for a job we've already filled. But if Fiona left . . .

Joanna: Have Personnel got copies?

Delia: Well, yes they have.

Joanna: Junk.

Delia: This is last year's monthly management accounts. But Accounts have got copies of this. And I know, junk. And memos about the safety inspection.

Joanna: For when?

Delia: Summer before last.

Joanna: Junk. Right, 'Managing Communications'.

Delia: Oh yes, that was very interesting.

Joanna: But will you ever actually read it?

Delia: It's very interesting.

Joanna: You didn't even know it was there. So how much would it matter if you lost it? And what is that pile?

Delia: Nothing.

Joanna: Come on. Everything you don't need might be hiding something you do need. What is that pile?

Delia: This is the 'Paperless Office' project . . .

Joanna: Well, why don't you do what it says? Come on. Give it to me. There, that didn't hurt, did it? Now we can really get going. And before you keep any piece of paper, ask youself:

1 Would I ever really have needed it?
2 Would it have mattered if I'd lost it?
3 Is someone else keeping a copy anyway? And
4 Do I need it all or just a bit of it?

Everything is presumed useless until it is proved useful.

And miraculously the office is rapidly transformed into a semblance of order.

Joanna: Right, that's better.

Delia finds her earring on a coffee table.

Delia: Oh look, there's the earring I lost at the Christmas party.
Joanna: That's pretty.
Delia: Yes, a lot of sentimental value in that.
Joanna: Right. Well, let's work backwards up the list and start with filing.
Delia: Er . . . before we actually start with the filing, what was it you were saying about some things we have to read? **Information**.
Joanna: Information. Right. What have you got to read?
Delia: Well, I've got to read these papers for the departmental meeting, definitely. I've got to read these job application forms and there was something over here . . . what was it? Oh yes! Yes, I've got to read these, the supervisors' reports, and I've got to read these articles on managing office services. That's good. Great. Right.
Joanna: What haven't you done?
Delia: What haven't I done? . . . you tell me.
Joanna: You haven't put them in order of priority. Some may be urgent, some not so urgent and some may be junk.
Delia: Right. Well, I've got to read the papers before the meeting; I've got to read these applications before the interviews and these . . .
Joanna: What's that one?
Delia: Well, this is an article on managing services.
Joanna: Aah! Are you ever going to read that?

Delia: Well . . . I might . . . if I had time. Oh, all right. Junk!

Joanna: Right. You see, there are two rules for information documents:

1 Only keep what you're really going to read, and
2 Put them in order of priority.

And so the documents are sorted, some junked.

Joanna: So, that just leaves us with filing and action. Let's . . .

Delia: Action. Let's do action first.

Joanna: All right. Pick out all the pieces of paper you need to do something about.

Delia: Yes, that's these on my desk. They're all here. I do have a system, you know.

Joanna: Nothing on the table? On the floor?

Delia: No . . . Well, actually yes. There is . . . this appraisal I've got to write up. Oh yes, and . . . that draft contract for the security people.

Joanna: That's the lot?

Delia: Absolutely.

Joanna: Good. Now. What can you get rid of?

Delia: Get rid of?

Joanna: Well, anything you need information on from other departments?

Delia: Well, yes, actually, there's the report on the electrical contracts. The House Engineer knows all about that.

Joanna: Well, never handle any piece of paper more than once. Make a note *on* it and send it off to him. Now, anything your colleagues can answer or give you draft replies on?

Delia: Well, I suppose . . . Accounts for the

payment queries. I mean, they incurred them. And Alison could check the draft security contract. But what if she forgets?

Joanna: Make a note to chase her for it. Right.

Delia: . . . That just leaves the hard core.

Joanna: So what's left is real work, right? Now, what's urgent?

Delia: . . . Well, I must get out the note on what to do while the Post Room's being refurbished. I must do that. I don't have to do the annual requisition order form for a week or two, that can go over there . . . and the agenda for the office planning meeting, I must do that.

Joanna: Great stuff. Keep going. And remember the rules for action documents:

1 Send them out with notes if you need facts or comments and give a deadline for response.
2 Make a note of the deadline and chase up late replies. And
3 Put the rest in priority order.

The action documents are collated.

Joanna: So that just leaves filing.

Delia: I'm sorry, I think I have to go now.

Joanna: Why?

Delia: I have to see my Head of Department.

Joanna: No, I am your Head of Department.

Delia: I didn't mean that – I meant I've got to make a phone call.

Joanna: You haven't got a hang-up about filing, have you?

Delia: No I haven't. That would just be stupid . . . wouldn't it?

Joanna: So, what are we going to talk about?

Delia: We're going to talk about . . . I can't say it.
Joanna: Filing!

Joanna goes to the filing cabinet and flings open the lid.

Joanna: Look, it's quite simple, filing . . . what . . . what on earth is this?
Delia: That's my laundry, I was going to do it on the way home. And that's my tea. I tried to begin with, I did, honestly I did.
Joanna: What went wrong?
Delia: Well, I just . . . I don't know. I just didn't know where anything was. I lost everything. Every time I filed it, I just lost it. So I had to just . . .
Joanna: What?
Delia: I had to throw the files away.
Joanna: How many files did you have?
Delia: Five.
Joanna: *Five*? Well, it's probably a very good job that you did throw them away. You can't do a job like this with just five files.
Delia: Do you know, that's what I found.
Joanna: What were the five files?
Delia: 'Alphabetical', 'General', 'Miscellaneous', 'Pending' . . . 'Other'.
Joanna: So where would budgets go?
Delia: Under 'B'. Or under 'General', or under 'Miscellaneous'.
Joanna: Not 'Other' then?
Delia: No, never under 'Other'. Sometimes under 'Pending', depending on . . .
Joanna: It didn't work?
Delia: No.
Joanna: Right. Let's start at the beginning. Separate the dead from the living. What's all this?

Delia: That's a feasibility study on contracting out house engineering. It'll be very useful for us if we look at it again in a year or two.

Joanna: So record and reference?

Delia: Exactly.

Joanna: So it's dead. For the moment, anyway.

Delia: I see what you're doing, yes.

Joanna: Any more like that?

Delia: You mean 'Bring out your dead!' Er . . . yes, I have actually got last year's electricity survey. That's the sort of thing, isn't it? And also the report on the new induction course. Under here somewhere are the quotes for the car park contract . . .

Joanna: Now, find me a living file. An active one.

Delia: Right. I know, yes, the Mail Room refurbishment and also the new central heating boiler . . .

Joanna: Good! Got it? With it?

Delia: Yes. It's brilliant.

Joanna: So let's get moving, and remember: Rule One for filing, separate dead from active files. And put dead ones out of the way. And do you think you can deal with Rule Two? It's to separate routine and project work.

Delia: Right. I can do that. Office Planning and meetings. Now that's routine and so are budgets. New staff directory – that's a project. So is reallocation of parking spaces. Invoice authorisation, that's routine. There.

Joanna: You see? The second rule of filing: separate routine files from project files. That also helps with your priorities. You can deal with routine work in next to no time.

Soon Delia's desk is more or less clear except for some odd scrappy bits of paper.

> **Joanna:** Do you need all these little bits of paper?
> **Delia:** Yes I do.
> **Joanna:** Well, why do you need this one?
> **Delia:** That reminds me to ring Parker and Gibbs.
> **Joanna:** And this?
> **Delia:** That one reminds me to fix a meeting with Marketing.
> **Joanna:** Then throw them away.
> **Delia:** No, I'll forget.
> **Joanna:** Well, write them on a 'to do' list first.
> **Delia:** On a what?
> **Joanna:** A 'to do' list. Things you've got to do today or tomorrow go on it. And the things you don't do today go into your diary or a bring-forward system filed under date or month . . . Now, what's this?
> **Delia:** That's a letter reminding me the vending machine people are coming at eleven o'clock on the 23rd.
> **Joanna:** Well, just put it in your diary.
> **Delia:** Good idea, I will. Diary . . .

Delia fishes a tiny diary from her handbag.

> **Joanna:** And you need a *real* diary with plenty of space for plenty of entries.
> **Delia:** I'll still need the letter, though, won't I?
> **Joanna:** No. Just put it in the 'bring-forward' system. That by the way is Rule Three. The third rule of filing is transfer 'reminder' documents to your 'to do' list, your diary and the bring-forward system, filed under date and month.

At last Delia's desk is clean.

Joanna: Well, we're nearly there. Last lap. You need lots and lots and lots of files.

Delia: . . . What sort?

Joanna: It doesn't matter. Let's start with the plain folders, that makes it easy, and we can put them in the cabinet later.

Delia: What, colour coded?

Joanna: If you like. I'd use buff ones for projects and label them.

Delia: Oh, I see and then you could use the blue ones for staff matters, and the red ones for accounts and budgets, the yellow ones for Office Planning meetings and departmental meetings, the green for invoices . . .

Joanna: Great. I'll just re-cap the four rules for filing documents:

1 Separate 'Dead' from 'Active' files.
2 Separate 'Routine' from 'Project' files.
3 Transfer reminders and documents to 'to do' list, diary and bring-forward system. And
4 Use plenty of file folders.

There is a knock. A post boy enters and leaves a pile of papers on Delia's desk.

Post boy: There's your post.

Delia: Right. I'll deal with that later.

Joanna: No, do it now. *Everything that comes in today must be dealt with today.* Go on. Remember the rules?

Delia: Right. Now, this has got to be junked. That is junk as well. Any more? No. Now secondly I'm going to put information documents aside for later reading. Those are information documents and so is that, so those can go there. And I'm going to junk any of the ones that I know I'm never really going to get round to . . . that's those. Now thirdly I'm going to send action documents out for others to deal with if I can. And I'm going to make a note to chase them all up on my 'to do' list. And put the rest in priority order. And four, filing. I'm going to transfer the reminders to my 'to do' list and to my diary . . . I'm going to have loads of files. It's easy peasy!

Joanna: Well? What do you think of your office now?

Delia: . . . It's all so bare, isn't it . . . so barren. I feel naked. Stark naked. I mean, what will people think when they walk in that door and see all this emptiness. They'll think I've got no work to do, that I'm just a nothing. And I am nothing but a nothing. You don't understand that all that paper was my job, it made me feel needed.

Delia buries her face in her hands. The phone rings. She picks it up.

Delia: Delia Dalton, Central Services. Yes, well, could you put it in writing . . . no, on second thoughts, drop in and talk about it. Well, ask him to put it in writing. No! Actually no, I'll go and see him! And forget the survey of user departments – I'll go round and talk to them myself as well . . . Well, why not today? Yes, of course I can. Oh and by the way you know this Parker and Gibbs proposal – let's go and talk to them as well. Look round their outfit . . . Great. 'Bye . . . I'm free! I'm free!

Delia picks up the folder Joanna has left on her shining clear desk.

Joanna: Free to be in the driving seat. Not just a Paper Processing Plant.

Delia (*looking at Joanna's folder*): Now then Joanna North. Can I have another look at my annual appraisal? Thanks. Oh it's a bit out of date, isn't it? And you know what we have to do with out-of-date documents? Into the bin . . .

Golden rules

1 Paperwork can create inefficiency.
2 The paper problem is everyone's responsibility.
3 Reorganise if you are a paper-slave.
4 If in doubt, junk it.
5 Presume everything is useless unless it is proved useful.
6 If you are sent a note make sure you reply on that note.
7 Routine and project files are always separate.
8 What comes in today must be dealt with today.

6 When can you start?

Good organisation can be introduced into company routines and into your own job. But a good manager knows that organisation starts before this can happen – with the **selection of staff**. For no company can be protected from the wrong person in the wrong job, and making sure this does not happen requires a special type of organised mind: one which operates like a detective; looks for clues; provides opportunities for justification or exposure; builds a picture like a jigsaw puzzle; is prepared to alter parts of the puzzle as new facts and circumstances come to light.

In fact it is no accident that the qualities of 'order and method' are associated with such luminaries as Hercule Poirot and Sherlock Holmes. They had no time for woolly thinking with muddled minds. The methodical approach to who did the job is no different from that which sets out to discover who is going to do it and do it best. So it is no accident either that, one dark, stormy rain-lashed foggy November night Sherlock Holmes is consulted about a particularly horrific case which he called 'The Unnatural Selection Mystery' . . .

Holmes: Pinnocle Systems Limited – the long-established purveyors of metal racking.
Wingit: Good Lord! . . . you really are brilliant!
Holmes: No, it says so on your card. Do pray be seated. That is Dr Watson's chair, who is already fourteen and three-quarter minutes late for tea . . . Well?
Wingit: Mr Holmes . . .
Holmes: Yes?
Wingit: It's about Pinnocle Systems.
Holmes: Go on.
Wingit: There's a . . . there's a jinx!
Holmes: A jinx?
Wingit: Every time I appoint a new Departmental Administrator something disastrous happens to them, disaster-wise.
Holmes: A jinx that goes with a job . . . intriguing.
Wingit: I mean, take Mary Morgan last year . . . She'd only been in the job a fortnight and then what happens? She goes barking mad. She's now confined to a padded cell with nothing but a plastic spoon to her name.
Holmes: Pray continue.

Wingit: And then Peter Parsons, doing so *well* until
. . . he *stabbed* himself in our office!

Holmes: Excellent, excellent.

Wingit: And then, four weeks ago, Dick Duffy took
the job. I walked into *his* office this morning . . .
And there he was. With a last message written on his
desk. It read 'I'm bored to death'. There's a jinx I
tell you, Mr Holmes! And people are beginning to
look at *me*, as if . . . as if they suspect foul play.

Holmes: And so they might.

Wingit: What?

Holmes: Had you thought where the jinx will strike
next?

Wingit: No . . . Why?

Holmes: Who appointed them all?

Wingit: Well, it's not my fault! Is it?

Holmes: Let's see. The last incumbent of the job
. . . Mr . . . ?

Wingit: Duffy. He was quite a find if you ask me.

Holmes: Why did you appoint him?

Wingit: Oh, he was quite clearly the best candidate
. . . interview-wise. I could see we were going to get
on from the moment we started talking . . .

The scene is described.

Wingit: Ah, Mr Duffy, I'm so pleased . . .

Duffy: Mr Wingit, I presume, and of HMS *Valium*,
if I'm not mistaken?

Wingit: Yes indeed!

Duffy: Type 150 Destroyer.

Wingit: Oh . . . are you a naval man?

Duffy: Short-term commission – submarines. I was
on the *Incorrigible*.

Wingit: Well, well, well . . .

Duffy: Could you tell me what the job actually involves?

Wingit: Oh virtually running the ship, my dear fellow. You'll be dealing with just about everything, information-wise. Plus a bit of liaison, minuting, report writing, you know the sort of thing . . . bit of this . . . bit of that . . . overall supervision of the database.

Wingit comes to the end of his story and turns to Holmes.

Wingit: I knew at once he'd be an excellent replacement for Peter Parsons. I liked the cut of his jib. Management experience . . . electronics business. Right person for the job, background-wise.

Holmes: And how did he settle in?

Wingit: He started out well enough, but then . . . well, he started clashing with Jill Siftwell, personality-wise.

Holmes: Who is Jill Siftwell?

Wingit: Our Credit Controller.

Holmes leans back, placing the tips of his fingers together. He has no difficulty in reconstructing a picture of what happened. In his mind he sees Jill Siftwell come into the office and start sorting through some papers. She is young, efficient and serious.

Siftwell: Dick, the Finance Director, is screaming for the draft accounts. I said this afternoon, all right?

Duffy: But I thought I was going to a credit control meeting.

Siftwell: No, that's *my* job.

Holmes envisages a deep sigh from Duffy, seeming to see him pick up the fruits of his morning's work – a chain of paper clips which he has carefully constructed. Holmes comes out of his reverie and looks accusingly at Wingit.

Holmes: You see?

Wingit: Yes . . . no.

Holmes: The job wasn't what he expected, was it? And *whose fault* is that?

Wingit: He should have known.

Holmes: How could he, if you didn't?

Wingit: I did! . . . Well . . . sort of . . .

Holmes: . . . If you are not to be the next victim, you are in urgent need of protection.

Wingit: Against what?

Holmes: Against picking the wrong people.

Wingit: And you are going to protect me?

Holmes: I can't. You must learn to protect yourself.

Wingit: But how?

Holmes: By breaking down the selection procedure into four logical steps.

Wingit: Right. With you.

Holmes: First of all you write down exactly what the job entails. You **define the job**.

Wingit: Define the job. Absolutely.

Holmes: Only then will you know the type of person you want to fill it. So then you **profile the person**.

Wingit: Profile the person. Jolly good wheeze.

Holmes: And having done that, you advertise clearly what the job is, and the sort of person you are looking for. You **communicate your requirements**.

Wingit: Communicate your . . . That's brilliant, brilliant, yes!

Holmes: And then you weed out the applications,

interview the short-list, and finally select the one person you want. In other words, **choose methodically**.

Wingit: Ah . . . but not necessarily in that order? I mean, order-wise?

Holmes: Imperatively in that order.

Wingit: Exactly. I quite agree with you.

Holmes: Those four steps, in that order, are the key to finding the right person for your job. It's elementary my dear . . . where *is* Watson? His tea's getting cold.

Wingit: Elementary. Yes.

Holmes: Well then, why didn't you follow them?

Wingit: Well, I'm a bit too busy for the elementary things.

Holmes: What did you appoint Dick Duffy to *do*?

Wingit: To replace Peter Parsons.

Holmes: Yes, but did you stop to ask yourself whether Mr Parsons *needed* replacing?

Wingit: I'm sorry?

Holmes: Was there a *job* for a Departmental Administrator? When someone leaves, that's your chance.

Wingit: Exactly.

Holmes: Chance to do what?

Wingit: Replace them? No, no – go on, tell me.

Holmes: Your chance to think.

Wingit: Well, I'm a bit busy for thinking.

Holmes: Well, then you have no protection against the jinx.

Wingit: But . . . All right, all right. I'll think . . . About what?

Holmes: About whether the same job still needs to be done. And in the same way.

Wingit: Well, I'm sure I must have considered all that.
Holmes: But did you discuss it with your colleagues? Jill Siftwell, perhaps?

Wingit thinks hard and aloud:

Siftwell: You must get someone with data input experience this time.
Wingit: But surely Peter wasn't doing so badly. With you and the others helping him out . . .
Siftwell: Yes, but we've all got our own jobs to do.
Wingit: He was good at chasing up slow payers.
Siftwell: But that's my section's job. We were treading on each other's toes. It was just the same with Margaret before him.
Wingit: No it wasn't . . . was it?

Holmes breaks in.

Holmes: You see? By thinking about it, you've realised you've got two people doing the same job.
Wingit: Ah! You mean that's why Dick and Jill clashed all the time?
Holmes: Quite so. Whereas if you'd thought clearly about the job . . .

Wingit thinks again:

Siftwell: The job we want somebody for is overall responsibility for data entry.
Wingit: Mm . . . And key tasks will include data entry, filing, production of all Accounts' printouts, maintenance of stationery, supplies-wise.
Siftwell: And that'll leave me free for credit references and debt-chasing.
Wingit: Much better. It sorts out that overlap.

Siftwell: And why don't you call the new job 'Admin Assistant'?

Wingit: Yes . . . yes, that might be wise . . . wise-wise.

The great detective intervenes with a masterly summary:

Holmes: You see, the first stage is: **Define the job.** Should you fill the old job? Should you create a new one? Or can you re-allocate the work-load? And now you've defined the job, next you have to think about the right sort of person to do it.

Wingit: Good idea. Go on.

Holmes: No. You go on. Think!

Wingit: Oh well . . . I suppose someone who's good at data entry.

Holmes: Aha! Already your sieving process has begun. That single requirement rules out a whole crowd of non-starters. Including . . .

Wingit: Dick Duffy?

Holmes: The type of person you DON'T want is as important as deciding the type you do. Think which skills and qualifications and experience are essential, and which aren't.

More thinking takes place.

Wingit: Well, we want somebody with computing qualifications . . .

Siftwell: No, we don't. Experience of data input is more to the point.

Wingit: Well . . . then at least some technical experience.

Siftwell: They only have to use the machine, not mend it.

Wingit: No, of course they don't, they don't have to

mend it, no . . . so basically all we need is keyboard skills. And accounts experience.

Siftwell: Well, not vital. But it would help. And the right kind of personality is important.

Wingit: Yes, we need somebody who's happy working on their own. What sort of age do you reckon? Not too young, I'd say.

Siftwell: Right. Someone who doesn't mind being office-bound. This could be an opportunity for a person with a disability. And one other thing. Can we *please* have a non-smoker?

Wingit: Oh, hear, hear! I'll add it to my list.

Another summary from Holmes as he defiantly puffs at his meerschaum.

Holmes: So – that's the second stage. **Profile the person**. First in terms of the skills, experience and qualifications you require. Then in terms of personality, compatible with the demands of the job, *and* the rest of the team. Now you know what the job is, and the kind of person you want for it. Was it for Mr Duffy?

Wingit: Jolly good chap.

Holmes: Yes. Jolly bad choice.

Wingit: Yes.

Holmes: Tell me, how did Pinnocle find Mr Duffy? Or rather, how did he find you?

Wingit: He answered our ad. 'Management team of large organisation requires go-ahead Departmental Administrator'. I was rather pleased with that. Rather a good advertisement, I thought.

Holmes: . . . Except that you didn't actually want a Departmental Administrator.

Wingit: No.

Holmes: Let alone a go-ahead one.

Wingit: No.

Holmes: Nor to be part of a management team.

Wingit: No. But it is a large organisation. Anyway, we got a terrific stack of replies.

Holmes: How terrific?

Wingit: So many, in fact, I had to stay late three nights on the trot just to get through them all. It was a great success.

Holmes: It was a total failure.

Wingit: Yes.

Holmes: A good advertisement deters everybody except the genuinely suitable. Would Duffy have replied to 'Large organisation requires Administration Assistant for filing, updating accounts information, and internal office duties. Non-smoker . . .'? You see, that rules the Duffys of this world out of the race. And the same clarity is needed if you advertise within your own organisation. A good advertisement does three quarters of your weeding out for you. Saves you the midnight oil. In any case you can always go to an employment agency.

Wingit: Ha! Don't talk to me about agencies. They can't possibly know what I'm looking for.

Holmes: Of course not. Unless you tell them.

Wingit: I do tell them!

Holmes: What do you tell them?

Wingit: I tell them I want someone really suitable.

Holmes: And what does that mean?

Wingit: Well, that's their job, isn't it?

Holmes: No.

Wingit: No.

Holmes: It's your job, so tell them *exactly*. Communicate your requirements precisely. Give

A good advertisement does three quarters
of your weeding out for you

them your job description and personal profile. Then
they can produce a short-list for you to interview. So,
remember to: **Communicate your requirements**.
Announce exactly what you are looking for by
advertising either externally, or internally . . . or by
thoroughly briefing an employment agency. Well,
suppose you've defined the job, you've profiled the
person, and you've communicated your
requirements. Now the interviews.

Wingit: Interviews. Yes. Oh actually I'm quite good
at those.

Holmes: Oh really? What do you do?

Wingit: Put them at their ease. Get them talking.
Keep it rattling along.

Holmes: So, what is the rule?

Wingit: The rule? Well . . . sort of . . . keep it going.

Holmes: The rule is 'choose methodically'.

Wingit: Yes, yes, well . . . that's what I meant. Choose methodically.

Holmes: Of course. And what is the foundation of a methodical choice?

Wingit: Give me a clue.

Holmes: Detectives are supposed to discover clues, not give them. I suppose you spend a lot of time looking at CVs?

Wingit: What's the use? They never tell you the things you want to know.

Holmes: Why can't you ever ask them? It's very very elementary. Send them an application form!

Wingit: But they send in all their details. Job record and all that.

Holmes: But that way you only get what your applicants *want* you to know. What *you* want to know and what *they* want to tell you aren't necessarily the same thing.

Wingit: Oh, I see. You mean sending them an application form forces them to answer my questions.

Holmes: Precisely. With your application form the elimination process can begin.

Wingit: Like a piece of detective work really.

Holmes: Exactly – painstaking scrutiny of evidence. We are in the same game, Mr Wingit. Except the kind of people *I'm* looking for don't usually write in offering to give themselves up. Now, let's have a bit more constructive thinking, may we?

Wingit obliges.

> **Wingit:** What do you think of Michael Middling?
> **Siftwell:** You ought to see him. He's an internal applicant.
> **Wingit:** Isn't he a bit young?
> **Siftwell:** A 'young man in a hurry'.
> **Wingit:** Mm. Must find out if he's not too ambitious for us. I'll make a note. Mark him as 'possible', will you?
> **Siftwell:** OK.
> **Wingit:** Now . . . Sheila Small.
> **Siftwell:** The one from the agency?
> **Wingit:** Looks a bit of a shrinking violet to me. Doesn't belong to any clubs or societies. No hobbies.
> **Siftwell:** But look at her experience. Ten years with one company.
> **Wingit:** Why do you suppose she left? 'Relocation'. I wonder what that means?
> **Siftwell:** You'd better ask her. We'll make her 'possible' too, yes?

The master summariser pronounces:

> **Holmes:** So you choose methodically, first by carefully scrutinising application forms and any other information the applicants supply. And next by preparing an interviewing plan and following it, which means preparing the questions you want to ask, and deciding the order in which you want to ask them.
> **Wingit:** I did that when I interviewed Mrs Small. I asked her some pretty tough questions, I can tell you.

Holmes conjures up the scene with no difficulty.

> **Wingit:** Did you ever have to work under pressure in

your last job?
Mrs Small: Oh yes.
Wingit: Mm . . . but was it real pressure?
Mrs Small: Oh yes.
Wingit: Good. Good . . .

And comments shrewdly.

> **Holmes:** Not very illuminating answers, are they?
> **Wingit:** Well no, I'm none the wiser.
> **Holmes:** That's because you phrased the questions
> wrongly. Ask *open* questions – get your candidate
> talking. *Think*. Think me through it.

Wingit does so.

> **Wingit:** You say your organisation is relocating,
> Sheila. What are your reasons for not moving with
> them?
> **Mrs Small:** They're relocating to Scotland, and I just
> can't move my elderly mum.
> **Wingit:** I see. When did you last work under
> pressure?
> **Mrs Small:** It must have been the day there was a
> power failure and the whole morning's input was
> wiped.
> **Wingit:** And how did you cope?
> **Mrs Small:** Well, everyone helped out, but it was
> very disruptive and I do like to know where I am.

Holmes breaks in.

> **Holmes:** And now Michael Middling. This is your
> chance to find out what an applicant's long-term
> ambitions are. Think on.

A new scene is thought through.

Wingit: Now Michael, what jobs have you applied for outside this company?

Middling: Oh . . . um . . . well, maybe one or two similar administrative posts.

Wingit: How many?

Middling: A few.

Wingit: What would you say if I suggested that maybe you're more anxious to be *out* of your present job than *into* this job?

Middling: I'm keen to get as much experience as possible.

Wingit: Yes. Well, I see you've been going to night school and increasing your qualifications. That's very commendable. Where do you see yourself in say . . . five years' time?

Middling: Well, obviously I don't want to be a junior clerk all my life . . . I'd like to think I was getting somewhere by then.

Holmes makes the point forcefully.

Holmes: You see? So, you've clarified that Michael really wouldn't be happy for long as an Administration Assistant. I wonder what that sort of interview would have exposed about our friend Mr Duffy?

Wingit: Ah, but he decided not to apply, didn't he – when I got the wording of the ad right.

Holmes: *He* did. But supposing a Duffy *had* managed to bluff his way right through to interview stage . . . it can happen. Now's your chance to spot it. Come along, Duffy *has* got through. Tell me about it.

The tale is told.

> **Wingit:** Dick, I see in one of your jobs you were
> 'Computer Salesperson of the Year'. What sort of
> competition was that? Was that a nationwide one,
> or . . .?
> **Duffy:** No – a company one.
> **Wingit:** Well, none the worse for that. And
> approximately how many other people were in the
> running for this title?
> **Duffy:** Er . . . oh, er . . . about half a dozen.
> **Wingit:** About?
> **Duffy:** Well, four really. Nearly four.
> **Wingit:** Three. Not a very big organisation then, this
> . . . Gleebe Electronics.
> **Duffy:** Not really. But it was quite successful.
> **Wingit:** But you've never actually done a routine
> office job, have you?

Holmes is satisfied.

> **Holmes:** . . . Right. Now, given the same choice
> again, which of those people would you now say was
> the right person for the job?
> **Wingit:** Well, Duffy's out for a start. And compared
> to Michael Middling . . .
> **Holmes:** But comparisons are odious, Mr Wingit.
> You should be measuring the candidates against the
> job, not against each other.
> **Wingit:** Well, I thought Michael Middling was young
> and keen, but the job wouldn't keep him interested
> for very long. I think I'll keep an eye on him –
> perhaps see if someone else can give him the next
> move he needs.
> **Holmes:** How about Sheila Small?

Wingit: Well, she'd be the one.

Holmes: Isn't she a bit lightweight?

Wingit: Well, we've got to choose somebody.

Holmes: No you haven't. If your selection procedure doesn't produce somebody right for the job, cut your losses – start all over again.

Wingit: But actually Mrs Small was right for it. She's reliable, steady, experienced . . .

Holmes: But she can't handle pressure.

Wingit: Ah, well, I've been thinking about that. Didn't we change the job specification so that Jill now takes on all the work which involves pressure?

Holmes: You spotted it. So, it is no longer a pressurised job.

Wingit: Right – it's a routine office job with fixed hours.

Holmes: Very good, Mr Wingit. You should be a detective. Case solved. Stage Four is: **Choose methodically** . . . Scrutinise applications carefully. Look for loopholes and things which the application forms are *not* telling . . . Interview searchingly . . . to clarify impressions and extract extra information. And measure candidates against the job, not against each other, considering them only in terms of their suitability for the job you want to be done.

Wingit: Mr Holmes, how can I thank you? I feel I have had a very narrow escape.

Holmes: Well, I told you that you were the one in danger.

Wingit: And I'm spared?

Holmes: No – only reprieved, unless you remember the steps.

Wingit: Yes, yes, of course. By the way, where is Dr Watson?

Dear Lord,
Let there be some doubt . . .

WHEN IN DOUBT FOLLOW YOUR IRRATIONAL INSTINCTS

Holmes: That, sir, remains a mystery. I may very well have to think about replacing him. So . . . what do I have to do?

Wingit: Ah! One. Define the job. When a vacancy occurs, ask yourself whether you should fill it or not, and whether you should consider creating a new one instead.

Holmes: Yes. The post needs to be filled.

Wingit: Two. Profile the person. Decide what kind of applicant you are seeking in terms of skill, experience, qualifications *and* personality.

Holmes: I am seeking an elderly buffoon with a medical qualification.

Wingit: Three. Communicate your requirements.
Whether you are advertising externally or internally,
or briefing an employment agency, say exactly what
the job is and what sort of person you require.

Holmes: I require a loyal, diligent, unimaginative GP
for twenty-four hours a day attendance on a great
genius.

Wingit: Four. Choose methodically. Get your
candidates to fill in application forms, and scrutinise
them carefully. Interview searchingly, using open
questions. And measure candidates against the job,
not against each other.

Holmes: We've defined the job so well there can only
be one applicant . . .

And at that moment the door opens.

Holmes: Ah . . . Watson!

Golden rules

1 Always define the job and profile the person as a starting point.
2 If someone leaves, ask if a replacement is necessary.
3 If someone leaves, ask if there is an opportunity to redefine the job.
4 Consider your colleagues first before you bring in an outsider.
5 Advertisements are supposed to invite suitable replies, not achieve maximum response.
6 Applicants must tell you what you want to know, not only what they want to tell you.
7 Measure candidates against the job, not each other.

7 The business letter business

Are your business letters clear, concise, polite and to the point? Lawyers and bureaucrats are, of course, notorious for making theirs incomprehensible, but that is no reason for the businessman or woman to follow suit. Moreover, letter-writing is *important*; not only because the letters are often an exchange of views and information – a dialogue – but because they are a permanent **record** about which there can be no misunderstanding. What you actually said or meant on the telephone can be the subject of argument, but no one can argue with what is in your letter. Moreover, you can copy a letter to others for information or action; not so with a phone call.

So, how would your letters stand up to scrutiny? Are you ever careless?

> Dear Sir,
> If you think our products are unsatisfactory you should see our manager.

> Dear Sir,
> In reply to your letter, I have already co-habited with your office, so far without result.

> Dear Sir,
> I am happy to provide Miss Jones with a reference. She has performed well in all positions in the bank, but has proved to perform particularly well over the counter.

Letter-writing is pretty well always a chore, and the business letter can be particularly hard, both for the receiver and the sender. One problem of a business letter is that you probably know the jargon of your trade, but does the person to whom you are writing know?

> Dear Sir,
> We should have the layouts for the Company Reports available next week. The illustration we were sent for the cover has been examined by our designers and they have decided to bleed from the bottom . . .

Such a letter *might* be sent to the Chief Executive of a large company who *might* not know that the designers intend to extend the illustration all the way down the cover without a margin!

Here is another example:

> Dear Sirs,
> Your letter of the 20th is to hand. With reference to your request for remuneration in regard to, and in the matter concerning, our recent acquisition of a number of items viz: thirty thousand three-centimetre self-adjusting grummet flanges. It is felt within these purlieus that in the majority of instances there is a negative aspect to their usefulness to this company so therefore I very much regret that no payment can, at this moment in time, be made. Our Chief Engineer is of the opinion that, and I concur that, the aforementioned thirty thousand three-centimetre self-adjusting grummet flanges are substantially inadequate in the fact that they are only 2.583 centimetres in diameter, and are not, one ventures to say, 'self-adjusting', and are not, you may

be surprised to learn, in fact grummet flanges, but, I am reliably informed, grummet filters. I look forward to an expression of your views on this strange state of affairs in subsequent correspondence.

Yours, etc.

Not so much trade jargon here; instead the writer has simply swallowed a dictionary and the recipient can't be expected to use one to understand 'negative aspect of their usefulness', or 'viz', or 'purlieus'. Is it any wonder that with such a convoluted style the company received filters instead of flanges? It will go out of business quickly if nobody understands what it wants.

Bosses probably have little idea of the contempt their letters, dictated or written, inspire in their secretaries.

Can it unscramble dictations?

There are those who dictate 'off the top of the head' and leave it to the secretary to sort out the resultant confusion

Here is a secretary describing a variety of letter-writers she has known: 'There's what you could call the "off the top of the head" ones. The "no preparation, eyes down, leave the secretary to sort it out later" type'. She recalls a typical example:

> **Businessman:** Dear whatever his name is, where the hell are our spare parts? God knows it's hard enough making ends meet without idiots like you screwing things up. So let's be having you pdq.
>   Yours, etc.
> Read that back, would you?
> **Secretary:** Dear Mr Foster, I'm sorry to inform you that the spare parts we ordered on form 02/593/27 have still not arrived. I'd be grateful to learn when we can expect them.
>   Yours sincerely,
> **Businessman:** Yes, that's fine.

Now an example of those who never use a short word when a long one will do:

> **Businessman:** It is commensurate with our policy relating to the contractual proviso of our purchasing agreements. We must conclude, however unaccommodating this might prove to you, that it is an ineluctable fact that credit is inextensible.
> **Secretary:** Isn't there a simpler way of saying 'pay up'?

Then, the letter-writer who is a frustrated editor, who strikes *after* the letter is typed:

> **Businessman:** Ah, that phrase should go there, now that really should go there – no I didn't mean denigrated – er what's a better way of saying it . . . put down? No – stet. As you were – denigrated. And make it 'Yours sincerely' – 'Yours faithfully' is too formal. Can you get it done straight away?

Secretary: I'm afraid not. I've got all the other letters you rewrote to type as well . . .

All a complete waste of time – the boss dictates, the secretary types, the boss rewrites, the secretary retypes.

So, how should a good business letter be written? It all boils down to two things – **work it out** and **keep it short**. Work out what you're going to say in advance, and make notes; then say it using short words, short sentences and short paragraphs. As closely as possible, stick to conventional language, not slang of course, but since you never say 'I feel it incumbent upon me as the recipient of your strictures', never *write* it either.

Now let's look at *what* is written in the good business letter. Imagine you have to write a letter to explain that an order of shirts from Japan won't be delivered to your customer because it has been held up at the docks . . .

> Dear Sirs,
> Re your esteemed favour of the 15th inst., I can offer you instead another line or two, one being more pricey than the other, as the shipment is held up at the docks by an Act of God. We're terribly sorry about this but we're both in the same boat. If we can't get the stuff, we can't get it to you owing to this cock-up at the docks. However, if you would like us to proceed with either Sylvester or Zabaglione items, as per catalogue in place of your Yamoko order, we would be pleased to proceed forthwith. Awaiting the favour of your esteemed command and assuring you of our best attention at all times,
> I remain, yours sincerely,

That's *all* wrong; in tone and content. Some of the faults we have already looked at – archaic Dickensian phrases, alternating with slang, 'Act of God' when what is meant is 'the Customs' and so on. But it is also wrong in simple construction. Remember a useful mnemonic: SCRAP, standing for Situation, Complication, Resolution, Action, Politeness. It will help you in many, many letters. The **Situation** is a statement of the fact or facts with which the letter is concerned; the **Complication** develops the facts and suggests a problem or asks a question; the **Resolution** suggests a solution; **Action** is a simple statement of alternatives – we know how we would like to proceed, in which case we will do such and such, but if this is unacceptable, then such and such will happen; **Politeness** is self-explanatory.

In the example above, the Situation is that an order

has been received and it hasn't arrived. The Complication is that the order is held up at the docks and the letter-writer doesn't know when it will be released; the Resolution is to offer what is available – other brands which have not been ordered; Action is a statement of the alternatives – will the customer wait for his order to be released or accept an alternative supply? Politeness, in this case, means making the letter more *personal*, and expressing fellow-feeling and goodwill.

	Dear Mr Parker,
	Yamoko Sports Shirts
Situation	I'm sorry we cannot delivery the Yamoko Sports Shirts you ordered on 15 January.
Complication	The department of Customs and Excise tell us that that shipment has been held up at the docks. They do not know when it will be released.
Resolution	As an alternative we can supply:

1 The locally-made Sylvester shirts at £206 per dozen, immediate delivery.
2 The Italian-made Zabaglione sports shirts at £244 per dozen, delivery within 48 hours.

Both Sylvester and Zabaglione are good value. They are available in a wide range of colours and sizes, and compare well with Yamoko sports shirts. I enclose our catalogue. Pages 15–17 will give you all the necessary information.

Action	I will telephone you early next week to find out which alternative you prefer.
Politeness	All good wishes.
	Yours sincerely,

Which of the letters would you prefer to have written? Which would you prefer to have *received*? Thinking of the latter is often a good guide to the former.

Think of the reactions of the recipient of the letter

To sum up:

Business letters should be simple, clear and to the point. The person you are writing to should understand what you are saying and so should you, so throw away the clichés and convolutions of the nineteenth century and stick to straightforward, uncluttered English.

Think about what you're going to write before you write it. Make notes. Be absolutely clear in your mind what you wish to say and how you intend to say it.

Remember SCRAP:
Situation – Complication – Resolution – Action – Politeness.

All business letters should be *logical, truthful, helpful* (where possible), and *to the point.* Clarity and Simplicity equal Efficiency.

Sample letters

Sales letter – Direct mail

Mr Frank N. Stein
Temples of Rest Ltd
Gravesend
Kent

Dear Mr Stein,

As a frequent organiser of conferences and meetings, you will be interested to hear about the Hades Hotel which has recently been extended to include a seminar suite.

We know that finding exactly the right facilities at the right price can present problems and believe we may now be able to help you solve them.

Situated only a few minutes' drive from Gravesend, the Hades Hotel can now offer a wide variety of meeting rooms to suit all requirements. The facilities are described in detail in the enclosed brochure. But why not come and see them for yourself?

My secretary will telephone you to arrange a convenient time. All our staff look forward to giving you a warm welcome.

I look forward to meeting you.

Yours sincerely,

Hilary James
Banqueting Manager

Sales letter – Direct Mail

Dear Pleasure Seeker,

Summer is nearly here and the evenings are getting longer. But when the summer is over, how will you store your garden furniture?

Manufacturers have at last realised that storage of garden furniture – when not in use in summer – is a problem for many people.

Many types of folding or knock-down furniture have now appeared on the market but we believe we have produced the ultimate answer.

Our new Awayday armchair is the best in foldability. It has four aluminium legs and one of the back uprights is shaped like an umbrella handle. Folded, the chair it is like a flat umbrella, only five inches in diameter. It weighs less than 4 lbs. Opened in a second, it becomes a chair with a seat, back, and arm-rests, all made of brightly striped nylon material in a choice of colours.

The demand for Awayday is likely to be overwhelming. We are, therefore, offering you the chance to order yours now. Just complete and return the reply paid coupon with your payment and your chairs will be with you within 28 days.

Best wishes for a wonderful summer!

Yours faithfully,

Sales letter – follow up

Miss J. Evans
43 Doncaster Road
Sheffield
South Yorkshire

Dear Miss Evans,

Thank you for your recent order for the suit advertised in our autumn catalogue.

This style, in the colour you requested, has proved to be very popular. I very much regret that we have sold our complete stock.

May I suggest that you look at the enclosed leaflet of new additions to our autumn range, several of which are available in the colour of your choice and at the same price. The style you requested is still available in navy blue and moss green.

Please mark your new selection on the enclosed form. Alternatively you may request a cash refund which will be sent to you by return.

I look forward to hearing from you.

Yours sincerely,

Valerie Pike
Sales Department

Letter of complaint

Dear Sirs,

5 Cedar Grove

I wrote to you on 10th August regarding a leak from the bathroom of the first floor flat in this property. The leak has caused considerable damage to the decorations of the ground floor flat.

I have not yet received a reply to my letter and the state of the decorations in the ground floor flat is deteriorating rapidly.

As this appears to be a structural defect for which the residents in the block have communal responsibility, I believe it is your role, as managing agents, to see that it is put right.

I should be grateful, therefore, if you would arrange for the leak to be repaired within the next three days. Otherwise I shall have to take legal action.

Thank you for your help. I look forward to a successful resolution of this matter.

Yours faithfully,

Answer to a complaint

Miss Mona Lot
3 St Georges Drive
Blank Town
Hampshire

Dear Miss Lot,

Thank you for telling us you have received an incorrect statement of account.

I regret that, although I have checked very thoroughly, I can find no trace of your payment.

May I suggest that you contact your bank to see whether your cheque has been cleared. If the cheque has been cleared I would be most grateful if you would tell me the date of payment from your bank and supply our batch number details. These details will have been stamped on the back of your cheque.

Assuming no clearance has been made, you would be advised to stop your cheque and supply us with a new cheque to clear your account.

Thank you for your help.

Yours sincerely,

Helen Watts
Customer Liaison Department

Answering an enquiry

Dear Mrs Sparks,

Thank you for your telephone enquiry about British schools in Japan.

I regret that the Japanese Embassy are unable to help in this respect. I can only suggest that you write, giving full details of your requirements, to the British Embassy in Tokyo. The address of the British Embassy is . . .

I am enclosing details of the Japanese education system which will give you details of our educational and cultural heritage.

I hope that you find a satisfactory solution to your problem and enjoy your stay in Japan.

Yours sincerely,

Confirmation

Channel Crossing Ltd
Ramsgate
Kent

Dear Sirs

Ref: SO41063

I telephoned you this morning to make a reservation for two passengers with car travelling between Dover and Boulogne.

Our arrangements have now changed. I wish to confirm the outward journey from Dover to Boulogne on Flight no.731 on Monday 13th September, 1982, but wish to cancel the return journey from Boulogne to Dover on Monday 27th September.

I enclose my cheque for £52.00 together with a completed booking form. I look forward to receiving confirmation and the tickets soon.

Thank you for your help.

Yours faithfully,

Debt chasing

Dear Mr Applegate,

It appears that we have not yet received payment of our invoice, no.9182, sent to you last December.

Our terms of business – stated on all our estimates and invoices – are 30 days net. Your invoice has now been outstanding for 90 days. It is our company policy to take legal action on all outstanding debts of this duration.

To avoid this embarrassing situation would you please send us a cheque by return. I am enclosing a copy of our invoice in case the original one has gone astray.

I look forward to receiving your payment by return.

Yours sincerely,

Job turn-down

Dear Ms Brown

Administrative Assistant To The Managing Director

Thank you for coming to see me last week in connection with your application for this position.

I have now interviewed all the candidates on our short list and regret that on this occasion your application was not successful.

There is another vacancy in the company for which I feel you may well be suited and I am enclosing details.

If this new vacancy is of interest, please ring me by Friday 14th June to arrange an appointment.

I look forward to hearing from you.

Yours sincerely,

Dorren Phillips
Personnel Manager

Punctuation

Punctuation is a problem for many letter writers – when to use commas, when not, and so on.

Many people make the mistake of inserting a comma, for example, when a pause seems necessary. This is the wrong approach. Although one of the purposes of punctuation is to supply the written word with the colour and emphasis that tone of voice, facial expression and gesture give to the spoken word, its main purpose is to enable the reader's mind to grasp the meaning of a phrase or sentence.

> Intellectually, spelling does not matter, but stops [punctuation] matter a great deal. If you are getting your commas, semi colons, and full stops wrong, it means you are not getting your thoughts right, and your mind is muddled. Punctuation is an invaluable aid to clear writing. (Dr Temple, Archbishop of York. See Eric Partridge: *Usage and Abusage*.)

So the rule is: **punctuate for meaning. If you keep to short sentences, you will not need more than commas and full stops, with the occasional question mark.**

Here are a few guidelines to help you.

The **full stop** ends any sentence. The question and exclamation marks carry their own full stop. Just as the question mark should be used only for questions, so the exclamation mark should be used only for exclamations.

The most common uses of the **comma** are:

1   to separate items on a list
    e.g. 'Our new range of T-shirts is available in red, blue, yellow, pink, and green.'

    NB: the comma is necessary before the 'and'. For example, note the difference between:

    'I wish to order black, and grey socks.'
    and 'I wish to order black and grey socks.'

    The exception is when a pair go together by association, e.g. birds and bees, gin and tonic, rag and bone.

2   to mark off clauses in a sentence
    e.g. 'As a frequent organiser of conferences and meetings, you will no doubt be interested to know . . .'

3   to replace brackets
    e.g. 'Your sales director, Marion Phillips, tells me that . . .'

4   around adverbial phrases at the beginning or in the middle of a sentence
    e.g. 'We have decided, therefore, to submit . . .'
    or 'However, I regret to inform you . . .'
    or 'Opened in a second, it becomes a . . .'
    or 'Situated only a few minutes' drive from Gravesend, the Hades Hotel can now offer . . .'

5   to separate clauses introduced by a relative pronoun.
    e.g. 'The men, who were carrying guns, were arrested . . .'
    means something entirely different from
    'The men who were carrying guns were arrested . . .'

In the latter case only those men carrying guns were arrested, whereas in the former case, the phrase 'who were carrying guns' merely describes the men by telling us that they were carrying guns.

Commonly mis-spelled words

abandon abandoned
absent absence
accommodate
accommodation
acquire
address
analyse
analysis
ancillary
apparent/ly
ascertain

belief believe
benefit benefited
biennial
bureau bureaux
business

commit committed
commitment
committee
comparison
conscious
consistence/cy
consistent
contemporary

co-operate
co-ordinate
correlate
courteous
courtesy
criticism
cumulative

decision
definite/ly
deter deterred
deterrent
develop/ment
disappoint/ment
disapprove/val
discrepancy
distributor

efficiency
efficient
eighth
embarrass/ment
erroneous
especially
essential
exaggerate

exercise
existence
extremely

feasible
February
foreign foreigner
fulfil fulfilled
fulfilment

grievance
guarantee

honour/able
honorary
humour humorous
hurriedly

implement
incompetent
independence
independent
influential
inseparable
irrelevant
irreparable
itinerary

liaison
loose loosen(s)
lose losing loser

maintenance
minimum

miscellaneous
movable

necessary
necessitate necessity
negotiate negotiable
negotiation
negligence negligent
negligible
noticeable

occasion/al/ly
occur occurred
occurrence
offered
omit omitted
omission

patience patient
permanent
permissible
personnel
practical
practice (noun)
practise (verb)
precede precedence
precedent
predominant
preference
prejudice
privilege
procedure
prominent
pursue

pursuant

receive
recommend/ation
refer referred
referring
referral referee
reference
relevant
relieved
remittance
resistance
responsibility

scarcely
seize
separate/ly separation
significance
significant
similar

statutory
succeed
success/ful
supersede

tariff
temporary
tendency
transferred

underrate
undoubtedly
until
usually

valuable

wholly
withhold

Letter layout

1 Follow the house rules on letter layout. For instance, whether or not to indent paragraphs, use reference numbers, reference initials, etc.
2 Check and follow any house rules on spelling, abbreviations, hyphenating words, letter endings, use of job titles, etc.
3 If no house rules exist as in points 1 and 2 above, use the following as guidelines:
   a) indent paragraphs if you have a company letterhead which is centred on the page. Letter

endings, i.e. name and job title, should then be centred.

b) range all copy to a straight left-hand margin if you have a letterhead which is 'ranged left'. Letter endings, i.e. name and job title, should then be ranged left too.

c) only hyphenate or break words where the hyphenation is natural or the break makes sense as two separate words/syllables on different lines, e.g. dis-similar, dis-jointed, sub-terranean.

4 Letters should be signed by an individual with the individual's name and job title clearly typed beneath the signature. Not:

a) per pro the XYZ organisation

b) for and on behalf of

The correct endings are as follows:

Yours sincerely

John Coates
Manager, Planning Development

Yours faithfully,

Sebastian Pound
Customer Accounts Supervisor

Golden rules

1 Business letters are a permanent record.
2 Avoid trade jargon where possible.
3 Clarity, simplicity, brevity are the hallmark of good business letters.
4 Think of the reactions of the recipient of a letter before you write or dictate it.
5 Plan difficult letters before you write or dictate.
6 Use the SCRAP method.
7 If you have to say no, try to add constructive alternatives.

Working With People

Do you know how to get your point of view
across effectively, without giving offence or
creating opposition, and knowing you are
being listened to properly? This is the art of
assertivenesss. Do you know how to get the
best out of your colleagues at meetings,
ensuring that valuable contributions from
others are encouraged in the best way? And
in those vital one-to-one exchanges can you
appraise others accurately so that both parties
benefit; or cope with discipline problems; or
deliver bad news constructively? This book is
about the human side of management,
recognising that working relationships are
the key to success.

Are You a Leader?

There was a General whose men said they
would follow him anywhere, but only out of
curiosity. Do you know where you are going
and do your colleagues know too? Taking
decisions at the right time; having the
courage *not* to take a decision; getting
commitment from others; running a meeting
for the benefit of all its members; focusing
not just on your business but the wider
context in which it operates – these are all
qualities of leadership in business. This book
shows how you as a manager can learn
leadership skills, changing your role from a
static to a dynamic one while enlisting the co-
operation of your colleagues at the same time.